Teaching Shakespeare

Teaching Matters

General Editors: Sydney Hill and Colin Reid

Teaching Shakespeare

Veronica O'Brien

University College, Dublin

Edward Arnold

First published 1982
by Edward Arnold (Publishers) Ltd
41 Bedford Square, London WC1B 3DQ

British Library Cataloguing in Publication Data

O'Brien, Veronica
Teaching Shakespeare.—(Teaching matters)
1. Shakespeare, William—Study and teaching
I. Title II. Series
822.3'3 PR2987

ISBN 0-7131-0725-1

In-house editor: Gayle Feldman

Text set in 10/11 Baskerville.
Printed by Butler & Tanner Ltd, Frome and London

General Editors' Preface

The books in this series provide information and advice on a wide range of educational issues for teachers who are busy, yet who are concerned to keep abreast of new developments.

The aim is practicality: slim volumes that are sources of authoritative help and swift reference, written and edited by people whose expertise in their field is backed up by experience of the everyday realities of school and classroom. The books are planned to cover well-defined topics relevant to schools in widely differing situations: subject teaching, curriculum development, areas of responsibility within schools, and the relationship of the school to the community. They are published at a time when there is a growing call for increased professional accountability in our primary and secondary schools. The 'in-service between covers' that characterizes these handbooks is designed to contribute to the vitality and development of schools and of the individuals within them.

This volume is remarkable for its author's sensitivity towards her subject combined with a very practical grasp of classroom realities, the needs and the difficulties. Through various imaginative strategies, teachers and pupils are invited to 'meet' Shakespeare in ways that are revealing, refreshing and informative. The skills needed to engage and sustain the interest and involvement of first years and sixth formers are described and explored in detail.

Miss O'Brien challenges many of the preconceptions of those who have taught the plays for many years, and her advice will be found especially helpful by the hesitant and the non-specialist. She illustrates her suggested approaches vividly, but avoids the trap of being over-prescriptive. Those who use it will form a 'creative relationship' with the book that will spark off individual attempts to make pupils' experiences of Shakespeare memorable and deep.

General Editors' Preface

Contents

Note: Where line references are given, the edition used is *The Signet Classic Shakespeare*, General Editor: Sylvan Barnet.

1

'Before the play is done'

This book is the outcome of years of enjoying Shakespeare in the company of all sorts of pupils—gifted and ordinary and slow, avid readers and children who had never read a full-length book, eager beginners and exam-ridden students. The pleasure began with the discovery that there need be no conflict between enjoying a play and learning to be articulate about it for the purposes of an examination. I remember my first anxious efforts: the cautious pace of the reading, the scene summaries, character sketches, explanations of dramatic technique. It was the excitement and confident understanding of one class during the Trial scene in *The Merchant of Venice* that made me question what I was doing and look for a way which would make that unforced attentiveness not a chance occurrence but a normal part of reading Shakespeare.

'Shakespeare has done it for you. Why not let him?' **(1)**. Granville-Barker's advice sums up the approach described in the following pages. It is true that teaching Shakespeare seems to present special difficulties in the classroom, given the gap between the complexity and density of the material and the intellectual and linguistic equipment of the pupils. But there are two vital facts to take into account. First, the very complexity means that there are several ways of responding to the plays; it is a commonplace that they can be enjoyed on a number of levels. Second, whatever their intellectual equipment, pupils have, like any audience, the emotional and imaginative equipment to enter the world of the play and to enjoy the experience made possible by the fact that it is a play. It is in this enjoyment that understanding begins.

The idea of growth is fundamental to the method, which exploits the complexity of the plays by leading the pupils over the years to an always deepening understanding as new levels are opened up with each new play or each rereading. Suspense of plot, how a play works, the relationship between character and action and theme, the nature of the language, approach to the meaning—these things come gradually, the challenge always matched to the pupils' actual ability to meet it. Fundamental also is the pupils' learning to record their knowledge: to build up their own 'aids' to the play, work which not only causes independent learning, but also treats exam competence as a natural result of study rather than its purpose.

The play in the classroom

We need not lament the fact that it is rarely possible for pupils to see the play in the theatre before reading it in the classroom. Indeed, seeing a performance first is not, I think, the right way to start. For beginners, the move from the immediacy of the stage performance to the unexpected difficulty of the play on the page can be the wrong kind of shock. There is, besides, the big disadvantage that the vital element of suspense is then missing from the classroom reading. For older, more experienced students, a live performance first can stimulate interest in a particular play. But, even with these students, there is much to be said for seeing a performance after, not before, a reading: they watch a play they know with more attentiveness, so that they see, hear, understand more. A television or videotape version should never precede an active classroom reading. The small screen translation is too reductive of the actual range of the original; the inevitable falsification of the stage-picture hinders rather than helps efforts to develop the skill of inward seeing while the play is being read.

The principle of approach is always the same: what is being explored is a play. The common objection that the classroom is an unnatural setting for Shakespeare overlooks the fact that no performance starts its life in the theatre. No play springs fully costumed, lit, set, to the stage. It is only to the playwright himself and to the live audience in the theatre that a play exists straightaway as a play. To those who work between the playwright and the audience it begins as a 'book', a text. Behind the stage performance lies a process in which producer and actors find out its shape, feel out the substantiality of character and incident, discover its *visibility*. They do so in conditions not dissimilar to those allowed by the classroom, conditions easy enough to reproduce there.

'Beginners please'

Teacher/producer and pupils/actors in a rehearsal room with the script of a new play in their hands. At all stages, from first form beginners to A level scholars, this is the starting point, though the way in which a given team goes to work will naturally vary over the years. There will be changes in the format of the script, changes in the way the producer seeks to engage attention, changes in the kind of seeing he hopes to cause, changes in the demands made on the group's critical collaboration. There will be changes in the number of available actors. Since all twelve year olds—even the shy ones—are convinced of their ability to take on a part, the whole of a junior class shares in the actual reading. Since only a proportion of sixteen-year-olds are so convinced, the reading is best done by volunteers. But, whatever shape work on the play eventually takes, whatever degree of sophistication of response is hoped for, the first step is a reading which is a *play*-reading. The classroom becomes a rehearsal room, which does not mean a radical rearrangement of the furniture; nothing more is needed than a reading area where the day's readers will sit. While a circular arrangement does contribute to the sense of being a group of actors, it is not a detail to worry about if school rules or classroom design make such an arrangement difficult. Much more important is that there should be continuity in the reading. Once the work has started, no other English work should interrupt it; all English periods should be given to the play until the reading is completed. A one-day-a-week approach breaks the rhythm of attention, reduces scene arrangement to the merely sequential and complicates the producer's job unnecessarily. The length of time the first reading takes again varies in the different stages. For instance, a first shot reading normally takes eight to ten periods; a middle stage reading usually takes nearly twice as long; a first reading with an experienced class may not take much longer than the actual playing time.

The way the teacher/producer approaches the new script is the key to success. 'Shakespeare has done it for you. Why not let him?' This does not mean that the producer's role is passive, but that it is in what Shakespeare has done, in the play itself, that the producer finds the way to mediate a play. As producer, the teacher has read the play and knows the production-slant he wants for it. The slant chosen will hold a first reading together. Coherence of intent is important there if that vital sense of 'play' is to be maintained. The production-slant is chosen on the basis of the teacher's knowledge of the group he is introducing to the play. He knows the level or levels of response they can reach, the kind of production likely to take this group into the play. There is only one slant, I think, which ought to be avoided, except perhaps with an advanced senior class: a reading which aims at understanding the play as an Elizabethan audience might have understood it. Such a reading would demand a sophisticated historical perspective foreign to a young audience, who anyway, like most adult audiences, take Shakespeare easily as contemporary. There is one big advantage the teacher/producer has over the professional producer: his production is essentially an ideal one, not hampered by problems of actual staging. To improve or refresh his ability to act as a producer guiding a play-reading, the teacher will find ideas in books which examine the stage-craft of the plays, or record the thinking of different producers, or describe actual performances(**2–13**). The Royal Shakespeare Company offers invaluable help in schools through workshops, seminars, working rehearsals(**14**).

The teacher/producer

The teacher/producer is a special kind of producer. He is not only helping a more or less inexperienced team to find their way into the life of characters in a certain dramatic situation whose story they are enacting; he is also helping them to be audience, to watch the enactment as well as take part in it. Extremely important in the classroom reading is the *dramatic visibility* it generates. When Shakespeare fails in the classroom, when the play remains cold on the page, when the reading is a continuous struggle to penetrate the incomprehensible, it is not primarily because the language is difficult. It is rather because not enough account is taken of how important the eye is in the dramatic experience. When a practised reader reads a play, his image-making faculty is as active as his logical understanding. It is this faculty that the teacher/producer seeks to set working during a reading. If he examines how a given play with which he is familiar lives in his mind, he will find there an inner stage on which the characters play out their story. From his sense of that inner stage, he stimulates the team's ability to build their own inner stages. In this work, the absence of an actual external stage and its paraphernalia is an asset, not an obstacle, for the absence means an invaluable freedom in visualization. It concentrates attention on the proper source of seeing, the script itself, Shakespeare's own stage-picture.

When thinking out the way he is going to direct a reading, the teacher/producer is always alert to the potential visibility of a line, a speech, a scene. It is this, and not paraphrasing difficult speeches, that governs preparation for the first reading. It is a mistake to over-estimate the pupils' quickness to see as well as read; this is a skill which needs development—particularly nowadays, when over-exposure to an image-filled world dulls rather than sharpens the habit of visualization from the word. The clearest indications can so easily be missed as the words are read:

> "Not on thy sole but on thy soul, harsh Jew,
> Thou mak'st thy knife keen" (*Merchant of Venice* IV. i)
> "Be thy tears wet? Yes, faith" (*King Lear* IV. vii)
> "My tables! meet it is I set it down" (*Hamlet* I. v)

When there is not a clear indication in the text, the visibility may be entirely blurred unless the producer is behaving as a producer should—evoking the image of *how* something is happening: the jerk of Brutus's head when he hears the shouting of the crowd; Hal's sudden freezing when his father accuses him of wanting his death; Portia's glance at Antonio when he is identified by the Duke.

A constant bringing to visibility is indispensable in the first shot at Shakespeare; it is an essential instrument in clearing the language-barrier.

The language-barrier

This brings us to what most of us see as the biggest problem—how to prevent the language from being an impenetrable barrier. The difficulty is that the language seems so remote from the language range of the children meeting the plays. It would be unrealistic to claim that there is no substance in the fear about the language; large numbers of children do not have the kind of previous language experience which makes Shakespeare's language immediately accessible. But this does not mean that they cannot gradually and pleasurably acquire that experience through Shakespeare himself.

The answer to the problem lies first in the fact that Shakespeare's language is the language of poetry. Experience with poetry in the classroom shows again and again the truth of Eliot's 'Poetry can communicate before it is understood'**(15)**. With Shakespeare's work, as with the work of any poet, trust in the power of the poetic word to strike home in the apparently most unlikely minds is essential to bringing about a happy encounter between a new audience and one of the plays. 'You can monkey about with clothes and settings as much as you like and the play will still pull you through. But touch the poetry and you are sunk'**(16)**. What we need to find is a way of helping the new audience to hear that poetry communicating itself. It cannot be a matter of simple exposure to the language, beginning at the beginning and going on till you come to the end. Such a method would hardly be more enlightening than it was for Alice listening to the White Rabbit's reading of the documentary evidence. There is a special problem with Shakespeare in that dramatic poetry demands from the beginning a grasp of narrative and a response to feeling. It is the producer's job to make that possible. He does not do so by careful paraphrase of speech after speech, or by summary of scene or act or play. Both methods, being non-dramatic, belonging to a different mode of learning, will effectively kill the play. The method one does use I call *chorus-work*, by which I mean a running commentary like that which a producer would naturally use during a preliminary read-through with the cast. In Chapter Two there is a detailed description of the method. What I want to stress now is that during the first reading it is our job to forestall incomprehension, not to test it; to keep the play moving easily and rapidly, not to allow Gradgrindery to turn the dramatic activity into the equivalent of construing a dead language.

It is a matter of trusting Shakespeare to 'do it for you', and trusting the pupils' capacity to enjoy having him do it. It is not pupils who import considerations which break contact with the actual experience of the play. They are seldom bothered, for instance, by improbabilities of plot. In the classroom, suspension of disbelief occurs naturally if the way the play is presented causes quick involvement. Junior pupils have a natural gift, too, for setting aside knowledge from other sources which might lessen the thrill. For example, I have taught *Julius Caesar* on several occasions to children who knew that Caesar was assassinated. Yet always they responded to the mounting tension in the scenes leading up to the assassination as if the outcome were in doubt. The capacity for this kind of enjoyment is not confined to junior pupils, and making room for its exercise goes on being important as play is added to play. There need never be a conflict between the pleasure and the work. It is enjoyment of the play in the first reading which determines the quality of further attention to it. Indeed, enjoyment makes pupils want to look more closely; it can be a motive at least as strong as the examination, and a very much more productive one.

2

First shot at Shakespeare

It is not possible to lay down a general rule about when pupils should read Shakespeare for the first time. Some are ready in the first year; most are ready in the second year; some are not ready till the third year. The problem is not one of emotional or intellectual maturity so much as of language reach. We all read against our previous experience, and much depends on the range of language experience the children have already had. The difficulty with Shakespeare is one of language pattern rather than of vocabulary. Twelve year olds who have enjoyed plenty of imaginative literature throughout childhood are accustomed to the diversity of pattern possible in language and are well able to take Shakespeare in the first or second year. But there are many twelve year olds who have not had enough of that kind of experience, and whose language range is still too narrow for them to respond happily to the unfamiliar patterns of Shakespeare's language. For such children the challenge had better be postponed until they have begun to move easily in the world of poem and story.

I realize that a number of factors make it difficult to offer Shakespeare in the first two years. But if the difficulties can be overcome, it is well worth-while making the effort. There are two very good reasons. Firstly, it is so satisfying an experience for both children and teachers. Secondly, it makes the later prescribed study of Shakespeare so very much easier. Pupils come to the play set for examination expecting to enjoy it and unafraid of the language. It may not, however, be possible to overcome the difficulties; suggestions are made in Chapter Three for approaching Shakespeare with pupils who meet him for the first time as part of a prescribed course.

The important thing about the first encounter is that it should succeed, should be so vigorous an experience that English is for the duration everyone's favourite subject. Well before the play is started at all, there needs to be a stirring of anticipatory excitement, designed to set up the expectation of a play and acting, to impress the notion that it is a *play* that is ahead rather than 'doing' Shakespeare, to give implicit reassurance that Shakespeare is not out of reach in spite of the look of the text. Indeed, it is unfortunate that so many children first meet Shakespeare in their school bags. For the reluctant pupil he is thus already another tedious educational obstacle; for the pupil of ordinary curiosity who opens the book, what he finds there is likely to be a closed theatre. The whole enterprise is much easier if the first sight of the text is in the illuminating company of the teacher/producer. There is one temptation that must, I think, be resisted in this preparation of a class for their first shot—the temptation to provide information about Shakespeare and the Elizabethan theatre. What matters now is that the children should accept him as contemporary; introducing history into the enterprise is to set up an unnecessary obstacle, to distance what should be near.

Choosing a play

The first question to settle is, what play? To succeed, the encounter must be swift and dramatic, so conducted that what is going on is always clear and attention-catching, that the language does not set up a distracting anxiety, that nothing is allowed to weaken the impact of the drama and the sense of being part of it. Now the level of enjoyment aimed at in this first shot is the first level of exciting action, so the play needs to have a story-line strong in suspense; the possibility of catastrophe is an important element. Again, the action needs to move fast so that suspension of disbelief can be held without check. The family of characters needs to be one where the grouping is clear and contrasts strongly marked; characters with whom the children can believe themselves able to identify—either superficially conforming to archetypes familiar to them in other forms of fiction, or having the surprise of novelty, as Shylock has in the elegant community of *The Merchant of Venice*. Now the comedies are not on the whole amenable to a first shot production. *A Midsummer Night's Dream*, for example, on grounds of both plot and language, is the wrong play for juniors to start with. They are at the very age to refuse suspension of disbelief in the convention of magic; it is not easy to keep the intricate machinery of plot moving without confusion; the poetry is too elaborately poetic to be readily accepted as dramatic. The brilliant ironies, the sophisticated play of wit of the later comedies, are too remote from what twelve year olds find funny. The major tragedies have certainly the element of catastrophe, and *Macbeth*, at least, can be made an enthralling experience for twelve year olds, but only at the expense of reducing the play to the level of exciting action, and potentially at the expense of later more mature responses to the play. *Romeo and Juliet*, in spite of the appeal of the *story* to adolescents, is not easy to handle with children who have no previous experience of Shakespeare. The run-in to the central action is too long; the language presents difficulties of a kind which imposes too slow a pace on the reading; beginners tend to be irritated rather than moved by the recurrence of accidents in the plot. The play works so well later that it is a pity to pre-empt enjoyment. As for the history plays, they introduce extraneous matter, which makes it difficult effectively to turn the classroom into a rehearsal room.

The two plays which fit the occasion best of all are *The Merchant of Venice* and *Julius Caesar. The Merchant*, as Granville-Barker puts it, is 'the simplest of plays, so long as we do not bedevil it with sophistries'**(17)**. It is easy for the teacher/producer to organize a reading where what happens next is of intense and sustained interest: the places of the story are readily imaginable by newcomers; there is the effective 'aid' of the character of Shylock, who from his first appearance communicates such a passion of aliveness that all the characters in his world become more substantially recognizable flesh and blood. As for *Julius Caesar*, the high danger in the first three acts, the speed at which events move, make it an ideal play for causing that quick involvement in the action so important in this first shot. Again, the plot-line is clear and uncomplicated by subplot, and the language has frequently that plainness which makes it possible for the teacher/producer to keep attention fastened on its comprehensibility. And this play has the huge advantage of the 'character' of the mob, which beginners can assume immediately and joyfully. A final point: both plays contain scenes well suited to a performance involving the whole group.

Preparing the text

Speed is extremely important if the enterprise is to succeed. For this reason, as well as for reasons of comprehensibility, an abridged version is essential for the first shot. The play should be so abridged that it can be read in 8–10 periods, not more, that is, than a fortnight. A practical method is not to use conventional texts, but to constitute special rehearsal scripts which are handed out each day to the class. It is much easier to maintain suspense if no one can say 'the-butler-did-it'. Few teaching experiences equal in pleasure that of reading *The Merchant of Venice* with a group of twelve year olds who don't know whether Antonio is saved. If any member of the class knows the story, some form of bribery or conspiracy of silence is justified!

Abridgement aims at bringing out the main story-line, focusing attention on action, emphasizing suspense—making it possible to keep that inner stage of the children's imagination a place where something is always happening. A sub-plot needs firm reduction; whole scenes can be omitted. The actual language is not tampered with, except in minor matters such as archaic exclamations or expletives—though these can be shifted on the spot or left to augment the exclamatory vocabulary of the readers. What one has in mind in making cuts—besides making the story-line stand out clearly—is the potential linguistic reach of the group. The question in this first shot is not 'Is this passage essential to a grasp of the play?' but 'Will this passage help *these* readers to keep in touch with what is happening?'. For example, in *The Merchant of Venice*, the Laban sequence (I.ii) would take far too much explanation to persuade beginners of the dramatic effectiveness of the argument by analogy used, and would slow the reading to a non-dramatic pace. But the "In such a night" sequence can be let flow without explaining the allusions at all. The situation—lovers and moonlight—and the lyricism of the verse communicate feeling rather as music does. All long speeches do not have to be reduced. In the early part of the play, when the mere look of a stretch of unbroken speech can cause anxiety, such speeches need more cutting than they do later when the group is caught up in the narrative and no longer afraid of not understanding. For example, the long speeches in the Brutus-Cassius dialogue (I.ii) need severe cutting, whereas Antony's orations to the mob need hardly any. Indeed, to shorten them blurs rather than makes clear what is going on. A mob busy responding in various dramatic ways to his eloquence doesn't want him to stop at all. Long speeches whose function is largely evocative of setting are unlikely, wherever they come, to fulfil their function with beginners and are better cut out. But the Duke's appeal to Shylock and Shylock's answer (IV.i), where the function is a heightening of dramatic tension, may not with many groups need any abridgement.

Shakespeare's prose at this stage causes more difficulty than his verse. For one reason, it is closer to the actual spoken language of his day and so less accessible. For another, there is missing the support of those non-lexical elements in the verse, continually working below the level of merely logical understanding, which communicate meaning so powerfully. This is not true of all the prose—the heightened individualized prose of Shylock, for instance, needs little cutting. But prose pitched in a lower key needs to be severely cut. Comic prose—unless the teacher is actor enough to translate it into visible clowning—is better cut altogether in the first shot. Jokes that need to be explained cease to be jokes.

Abridgement: The Merchant of Venice Act I

Cut Scene 1: Salerio 9–14 (i.e. 'argosies' image); Solanio 19–22; Salerio 25–39; Solanio 50–56. Use running commentary for entry of Bassanio, Lorenzo, Gratiano, and exit of Salerio and Solanio. Pick up at Gratiano "You look not well ...". Cut only Gratiano 74–75, 101–102. Running commentary for exit of Gratiano and Lorenzo. Bassanio 115–118, 126–130, 140–152; Antonio 153–157 (i.e. Antonio continues straight from "Lie all unlocked to your occasions" to "Then do but say to me what I should do ...").

Cut Scene ii: Entire scene. Replace by producer narrative.

Cut Scene iii: Shylock 17–25; Shylock *et al.* 65–99 (i.e. the Laban sequence); Antonio 130–134; Shylock 157–167.

Abridgement: Julius Caesar Act I

Cut Scene i: Marullus; Flavius 56–63; Marullus 75–78.

Cut Scene ii: Cassius 35–36; Brutus 42–47; Cassius 48–50, 54–58, 71–78, 112–115, 119–131, 139–153; Caesar 201–207; Brutus and Cassius 292–309 (i.e. retain Casca's account of offering of crown; replace final Brutus-Cassius dialogue by recapitulation of what Cassius is working towards and how Brutus feels about it).

Cut Scene iii: Casca 11–13, 26–32; Cicero 34–35; Cassius 64–68, 80–84, 91–98, 106–111, 126–130; Casca 157–160; Cassius 161–164.

Introducing the play

Since success depends on the rapid engagement and sustaining of interest, it is necessary to make sure that there will be as little interruption in the work as possible, to choose a fortnight when the school programme doesn't include such occasions as sportsday or half-term break, and when it is possible to give all English periods to the play.

The first period is given to clearing the way for the reading. However much interest has been awakened, there are always last-minute doubts and alarms to be dealt with. The producer/drama-group situation is established. A decision is taken on how to arrange the classroom for the reading: an area where the day's readers will sit, how best to dispose the seats for the audience. Then comes the specific introduction. Very little background information is needed for *The Merchant of Venice*. Indeed, the title indicates how much: the world of business, of overseas trading in sailing-ships, of a busy port; the place, Venice—thanks to TV—is seldom a problem. A little more background information is needed for *Julius Caesar*, because of the political content. This is given in terms of the pupils' political knowledge. Children nowadays can't help knowing something of the struggle for power, the party struggle, the see-saw of who's up, who's down. The producer might explore their knowledge of dictatorship, though this can be left till later. The basic fact that the play starts in the middle of a shift of power is what he wants to get in now. A coup has brought Caesar to power and displaced Pompey. There is no need to go into detail; the political machinery of the play becomes visible in the play itself.

Names of the main characters are introduced orally. Names of lesser characters are left till they appear in the reading. Tweedledum and Tweedledee names—the Sal/Sol group in *The Merchant*, for instance—are treated as lightly as Shakespeare treats them. So are the names of characters whose appearance is as brief as that of Marullus and Flavius in *Julius Caesar*.

Part of the visibility which the producer will aim at making possible throughout the reading will be that of place. For beginners it is not stylized setting which is in question. What the producer tries to do is to stimulate the group into creating and holding an image of the places of the story. For this purpose, the aural aid of the producer's voice evoking the look and feel and life of a particular setting is much more provocative of active collaboration than the visual aid of film or picture. The former is flexible, encourages a greater freedom of individual response, and, since it is always available, is much better able to meet the immediate demand than the latter. Most important, the producer's voice is a living aid. In the introductory period, the producer begins this part of his work by giving general information about where the action happens, inviting the children to pool their knowledge, aiming at bringing to the forefront of consciousness their notions of ancient Rome or the colour and light of Italian cities.

The first day

In the next period the scripts are handed out and play-reading begins. The producer has timed the day's reading so that the first scene will fit into the period with time to spare. (Scene i in *Julius Caesar* corresponds to scenes i and ii in the full text.) If possible, a double English period should be chosen for the first scene, so that there is no danger of a mistiming which would cause the reading to be interrupted at an awkward point. The first scene is a one-man show, the producer playing all the parts. The producer needs the space to establish himself in the multiple personality he will enact throughout—storyteller, continuity man, stage-manager conjuring up props out of mid-air, lighting expert, sound-effects man, setter of pace, illuminator of mood and action. The group needs to be accustomed from the beginning to his way of behaving. On this first day the producer has the vitally important and delicate task of slipping the group past the language-barrier; this cannot be done using unskilled readers. All the previous building-up of interest and expectation can be destroyed by the shock of a language so unfamiliar as to seem unmanageable. So the producer slips the group past the barrier by his own reading. It is at this stage largely a matter of bluffing them into thinking they understand, by assuming the mediatory role of producer, not literary explicator. It is as producer that one breaks the code of the text, as a natural part of a producer's job.

The language problem is overcome by never being allowed to obtrude as a problem. Throughout the reading the producer forestalls the children's finding the language incomprehensible by acting as a sort of chorus. He does not say 'The next lines mean . . .', but works in what they mean in his role as producer, using an informal idiom, so that the children know what is said before they hear Shakespeare say it. They do hear Shakespeare's language, but they hear it already understanding its content sufficiently to believe they understand the words. The producer's parallel chorus is not a substitute for Shakespeare, and it is never a word-for-word paraphrase; there is no need to explain every item, even of an abridged version. Most important, it comes dramatically as a natural part of the way the producer brings the script to acting life. The mode is adapted to the group, the informality of comment is matched to the mood, the tone of what is coming. Thus—Cassius watching the effect his words are having on Brutus; Brutus half-listening, his body stiffening at another roar from the crowd. Shylock watching Antonio's arrival while pretending to be doing sums; standing apart, hating this Christian who doesn't charge interest, who mocks Jewish customs; his feeling of hatred so intense that it comes straight across to the audience, while the two friends greet one another. Always, in fact, not only what's being said but also how—the tone, the pause, the turn of the head.

Handling the first scene

The Merchant of Venice I. i. (Antonio, Bassanio, Lorenzo, Gratiano)
Setting the scene: Evocation of a busy street in Venice. Italian afternoon. Palaces and bridges. Noise and bustle at the central landing-place, coming and going of carriers, etc. Small groups of merchants doing business. Gondola arriving at landing-stage with three richly-dressed young men, one of whom has just snatched the gondolier's pole and is amusing his companions with his efforts to land the gondola. Impossible to hear what anyone is saying...
Moving into script: Those three men near the archway—two talking urgently to the third who is prosperous-looking, not so gaily dressed. That's Antonio. He's shaking his head, holding up his hand to stop their chatter. Now he's saying something, can just catch the words. Producer glosses script: Antonio doesn't know why he's so depressed, why he's such poor company today ... Producer slips into opening lines "In sooth ... I am to know".

Others try to persuade him that he's anxious about his ships at sea. A storm at sea could mean he'd lose every penny. (Sailing-ships more risky than modern cargo-boats.) They would be just as anxious if *they* had a fortune "tossing on the ocean", wouldn't be able to think of anything else ... Producer reads abridged version of Solanio/Salerio speeches. But Antonio says they're wrong ... It's not that, not business. He hasn't all his eggs in one basket. Producer reads script and continues without chorus intervention through 'in love' argument, and 'sad because not merry' argument—abridged version. Conversation interrupted by the three from the gondola, Bassanio, Lorenzo, Gratiano—he's the one who snatched the gondolier's pole. Still laughing at Gratiano's play-acting as they greet the other three. The text of the greeting and exit of Sol/Sal can be retained but not necessarily read; running commentary may be sufficient.

While that has been going on, Gratiano has been peering at Antonio, walking round him as if he wanted to examine him from every angle. Antonio hasn't taken any notice of him (or he has—producer's choice) but has been watching Bassanio and the others. Now Gratiano stands up close to him, shakes his head, declares that he's looking poorly. Producer reads speech and Antonio's answer. Gratiano skips back from him, does a half-turn and races into speech. The "Let me play the fool" speech can be given whole, the producer acting it out rather than using prefatory comment; throwing in occasional asides as explanation without changing speed to do so. For instance, "his grandsire cut in alabaster" can be glossed as 'cold as a statue of his grandfather'; "sort of men ... bark" as 'the kind of people who keep silent to give the impression of being full of deep thoughts; if they opened their mouths they'd be sure to say something stupid'. The speech does not need detailed explanation and is a manageable initiation into the run of Shakespeare's metrics. It has the rhythmic vigour to get the sound of the iambics on to the listeners' ears naturally. The transition to the Antonio/Bassanio dialogue would be a mixture of script and producer's chorus. For the dialogue proper, the strategy would be similar to that used for the opening sequence—chorus comment and actual text. The Colchos image is retained. With some classes it may be necessary to do no more than to remind them of the story of the Golden Fleece. If the children have never heard of the legend, a very brief indication of the quest can be given, or, if the producer thinks fit, the allusion can be cut. Antonio's promise to borrow money should cause some surprise in the light of what he has said earlier, and is a point for discussion since it is the first sign of danger.

Scene ii is cut. The producer acting as *storyteller* explains Portia's unusual position, the conditions of her father's will and the many suitors who lose their nerve when they hear these conditions. Emphasis would be laid also on the kind of place Belmont is and its distance from Venice.

Julius Caesar I. i and ii combined (Mob, Caesar, Mark Antony, Brutus, Cassius, Casca)

Setting the scene: Public holiday in Rome. Citizens enjoying a day out to celebrate Caesar's triumph over Pompey and his coming to power. Streets crowded and cheerful, statues decorated, fountains full on. People in best clothes singing, shouting, drinking. Some details of their activity: a man climbing a statue to hang a garland round its neck, cheered on by his friends (he can fall into the water); roars of laughter from a group where a man is telling funny stories.

Moving into script: Two men come round the corner (their names don't matter; they don't appear again), different from the crowd, serious, angry-looking. One pulls a garland from a statue and throws it aside. No one takes any notice. The two confer, come to a decision, begin to push their way into the crowd, shouting, calling for attention. Still no one takes any notice. One of them climbs on to the base of a statue near where the man is telling funny stories and begins to shout for silence. The joke-teller (he is of course the Cobbler) stops to look, and those around him look too. Noise dies down; what is being shouted can now be heard. Producer glosses script: the newcomer is telling the crowd to go home; this isn't a proper holiday; they have no right to be roaming the streets in holiday clothes; they ought to be wearing working clothes. Producer reads opening lines: "Hence! Home ...". For the sequence with the Cobbler a mixture of text and gloss is used. The puns here are of a kind popular with children. The sequence needs to be taken rapidly, depending on a certain clowning to get the point home, drawing the group into crowd-reaction.

Cobbler shifts the tone: he sees Marullus's anger and stops teasing. Marullus and Flavius try to stir up the crowd's sympathy for the dead Pompey. It's not so long ago that they came to cheer Pompey, not Caesar. Marullus's speech (cut version) is a good initiation into the rhetoric of the play. Delivery should be declamatory. The speech is followed by the muttering dispersal of the crowd, while Marullus and Flavius decide to clear away as many signs of festivity as they can. It is important to keep stirring visualization ability here, to stress the sense of city streets. Now from another direction come sounds of cheering and the procession enters. Caesar is played with stressed arrogance; the group is drawn into providing crowd noises. Give them Caesar's name to shout, with what additions they choose. The Lupercal sequence needs a little explanation: a festival procession to bring good fortune; Mark Antony's being one of those who run through streets with switch or thong; Caesar's desire for a son. The Soothsayer's strange interruption (in a chanting voice) rises above the general noise. There are two elements to stress in this sequence: the excitement of the people and the reiteration of Caesar's name. The moving off of the procession and the emptying of the street need vivid evocation.

Cuts in the Brutus/Cassius dialogue aim at making clear Cassius' resentment of Caesar, his accusing Caesar of having delusions of divinity, his manipulation of Brutus, and Brutus's being in two minds. Certain cuts can be replaced by the significant pause, e.g. "Tell me, good Brutus, can you see your face?" comes out of a pause. Cassius, watching Brutus, *thinks* before he speaks. The words carry surprise by their apparent lack of connection with what Brutus has said. The shouts of the distant crowd and their effect on Brutus are given strong value. Forestalling of incomprehension is important in the dialogue. The swimming contest passage can come without much choric intervention, but the Colossus passage needs producer pre-illumination. When Brutus says he is afraid more honours are being "heaped on Caesar", Cassius jumps at the chance to get what he wants—to work up Brutus against Caesar. So he lays it on about Caesar's dangerous pride—he is like a huge statue the rest of men have to crawl under. (The Colossus was a huge statue built astride a harbour.) There's room for no one else now in Rome except Caesar. And it works. Brutus does listen. He himself has begun to have the same notions about Caesar . . .

If it is a double period, there is normally time to go right through to Casca's account of the crowning. In this sequence, the parts of Brutus and Cassius can be taken by pupils, the producer playing Casca with strong emphasis on the running commentary element in the account.

How the reading proceeds

After the one-man show of the first scene, the children become the readers. A rota is worked out so that all get their chance. It can be so organized that there is always a mixture of talent in the day's reading. Furthermore, the producer will often be quite naturally one of the readers, or he may start off a character before handing it to a pupil. He is always discreetly present, again as producer, to prop up a stumbling reader. He does not lose sight of his multiple functions. He remains always on the alert to forestall incomprehension, to prevent the flatness that results from confusion. The amount of forestalling needed usually decreases as the reading goes on, but it can never be withdrawn altogether. Sometimes there are stretches when there is very little need for this kind of intervention: the Mob scene in *Julius Caesar*; the Trial scene in *The Merchant of Venice* after Portia's entrance. It is not that the pupils understand everything, but that their sense of what is going on causes them to predict correctly. Understanding depends on the producer's vigour in setting the scene, creating the atmosphere, generating excitement in the action. One needs to start *every* reading by stirring imaginative collaboration with setting and mood. The more clearly the readers are 'seeing', the less they worry about not understanding. Stressing visible action diverts attention from the difficulties of the lexical surface, and at this first level that is what matters. Planning each day's reading is essential; it is the teacher/producer's visualization that facilitates the children's. Planning will naturally include a logical starting and stopping point; the more often this means a cliff-hanger, the better.

If school rules demand written homework, there are ways of answering the demand which do not spoil the sense of a play-reading. One way is to set a 'telegram' competition going. The events in the day's reading are recorded in telegram form by each pupil. At the end of the play, the pupil whose telegrams have cost least and yet are clear is the winner. (If the play is *The Merchant* there can be two correspondents, one in Venice and the other in Belmont.) Other forms are the newspaper headline or the descriptive title for a section. The challenge of this kind of work, besides being interesting, is better training in recognizing essentials than the scene summary provides.

In this first encounter, what one wants to generate is the excitement of sharing in a dramatic fiction and the confidence which comes from the illusion of moving easily in rich, satisfying language. My experience is that if one does not draw attention explicitly to the fact that the language is metrical, pupils take the fact as natural. Nor is the ease of movement entirely an illusion. There *is* understanding, just as there is understanding of other forms of poetic language. That it is not the understanding of the annotator does not make it less valuable or true. A class that is caught up in a play can surprise by its perceptiveness about the language. 'The way Shylock says *sufficient* when he's talking about the bond—well, he doesn't only mean Antonio has enough money. He means if he can catch Antonio, it'll do for his revenge on all those Christians.' And I don't think I have ever had a class which needed to be prompted into recognizing the varying significance of Antony's reiteration of "Brutus is an honourable man".

Acting Shakespeare

When the reading is completed, the natural follow-up is acting—either part of the play in which the whole class can be involved, or the whole play with different groups acting different sections. The former leads to better theatre, objectively; twelve year olds can give a good performance of the Trial scene in *The Merchant of Venice* or the Mob scene in *Julius Caesar*. As in professional production, the crowd is encouraged to be actively involved in the scene, each member finding a specific role for himself. Acting the whole play gives scope to a lively class for independent realization of the inner stage; but the resulting performance is likely to be a mixture of styles as well as talents and can be confusing for an audience.

There is no need for elaborate equipment. Costumes can be rudimentary, props cut to a minimum, setting a matter only of enough space. The group will want an audience, which should be an audience of its peers. Whether the teacher continues as producer or leaves it to the children is a matter of choice. He will normally find himself retained in an advisory capacity, even if the production is in the hands of the children. The challenge of actual performance brings them into a new relationship with the script, into what might be described as the first stage of a critical response to what they find there. While they treat much of the speech and action as if it were perfectly within their comprehension—which confidence is the natural result of a successful play-reading—there is also a certain amount of 'What does this bit mean?' 'How should it be said?' The distinctive natural characteristic of children's acting is enthusiastic involvement, and it is this rather than subtlety of interpretation that is to be encouraged. Very important is the involvement and individual role-making of the members of the crowd. The end performance should be energetic rather than elegant, swift rather than precise; and it is not an occasion for interfering with personal accent.

When a group is caught up in a performance, they can surprise even themselves by intuitively right impromptu stage business. For instance, I remember the exit of Shylock in the Trial scene in the performances of two different groups. One Shylock responded to Gratiano's taunting by suddenly stumbling and falling. The crowd laughed. The other Shylock responded by turning on Gratiano with raised knife. The crowd was immediately silent. The interesting thing is that neither bit of business had occurred during rehearsal. Each came out of not simply the individual actor's absorption in his role but the involvement of the whole group.

A Shakespeare festival in which different streams or sets present their version of a scene is always popular. In one school the discovery of a small statue of Shakespeare during a clearing-out of junk under the stage led to the setting up of 'The Shakespeare Trophy' as an annual event for first year pupils. It has meant that all first year pupils, whatever ability range they have been slotted into, meet as equals in enjoyment of Shakespeare.

3

Shakespeare prescribed: the first reading

Pupils who have enjoyed their first encounter with Shakespeare are well-disposed to take him in their stride when they next encounter him, usually as a text on an examination course. Clearly, it is important that expectation of enjoyment should not be disappointed by the way a new play is approached. The fact that a play is prescribed is not a signal for treating it as material for paraphrase, by beginning on a patient gnawing through the text inch by inch. The advance in response, in understanding, that one hopes to bring about in the second encounter, can occur only if the play as play is not lost sight of. Thus, anxiety about eventual exam-competence should not lead to any version of the 'next-please' routine: Pupil A reads a passage, Pupil B or C or D is asked to explain, teacher eventually gives explanation, and all pupils scribble in the margin. Such an approach has in it the seeds of its own failure. The slowing of pace obscures the drama; interest—if it survives at all—is focused on the wrong things; the parts are so widely separated that there cannot occur any spontaneous recognition of how they all contribute to a living dramatic whole.

For many pupils the prescribed play may be the first encounter with Shakespeare. In this situation, the approach will depend on the general ability level of the class. If the pupils' language range is limited, it is wise to use an abridged version for the first reading, and the approach described in Chapter Two. The emphasis throughout would be adapted to the greater dignity of fourteen or fifteen year olds. Pupils whose language range is wider can be taken much further even in the first reading. The play need not be abridged for these readers. The reading starts on the level of exciting action, but the producer begins to open other levels as soon as it is clear that the pupils are enjoying the experience. It is usually possible after the first act to work in the same way as with pupils who are reading their second play.

The first reading of a prescribed play is again conducted as a play-reading. The teacher is still producer, illuminating, supporting, forestalling incomprehension, making sure that his production has visibility as well as narrative clarity, and that it moves fast enough to hold attention. There is no need to explain every line; the important thing is imaginative involvement of a kind that lasts. The first level of enjoyment—the excitement of action—is still part of that imaginative involvement as it always will be. A fully developed response to Shakespeare is, after all, still to hold one's breath at the Murder scene in *Macbeth* or the Awakening scene in *King Lear*.

The text will be a more or less full text, but in the first reading at least the teacher/producer will do a certain amount of judicious cutting where there is danger of flagging interest. Again, the text is likely to have some critical apparatus. How to use this apparatus is something to be taught in its place, which is certainly not during the play-reading. The notes should not be allowed to clutter up access to the play itself, should not appear to the pupils as intrinsic to it, which would be a likely result of too early a use of them. The play may very well be the first long work of a set literature course that is embarked upon; it does make a good starting point for a class that has been exhilarated by a previous happy experience of Shakespeare. This is not the moment for undermining confidence by an approach which suggests that Shakespeare is very much more difficult than he seemed the first time. As with every work of literature, from short poem to long novel, the approach at this stage should imply that the pupils need no more than their own wits and the work of literature; the unspoken assumption is that the work is something they are capable of taking into their possession with interest and satisfaction.

Opening further levels of response

Eventually, attention to the prescribed play will become study of a number of aspects, but this is not how it will start. It is a mistake to try to accommodate too much at once. Much better to 'let Shakespeare do it for you' and to wait until he has done it before demanding organized reflection on the parts. During the play-reading stage, the pupils are explicitly challenged to be alert to certain features of what they are taking part in and watching. The point is that when young readers are confronted with a major adult work, a focus of attention is needed, a clear direction of observation which gives them a hold on the complexity. What we now want to happen is the beginning of independent recognitions, and the way to this is the habit of noticing. Set them watching for specific things and the result is often the spontaneous noticing of other things.

Since it is extremely important to reinforce the pupils' sense of the dramatic, to prevent their seeing the text of a play as they see the text of a novel, the specific challenge set should be essentially theatrical. What is aimed at now is sharpening awareness of how a play works on an audience. The specific aspect to which attention is turned is related to the production-slant chosen, a slant which will not this time be simply that of emphasizing excitement of action. As a general rule the challenge is oral, a matter of informal class discussion. Some written work is suitable, however: a start can be made on keeping a note-book, provided that this does not slow the reading too much or obscure the 'seeing' of the play as play. Indeed, note-book work which is clearly based on the production-slant can help to counter the unnaturally long intervals between the parts of the play. See Chapter Four for examples.

Some examples of opening new levels

The Merchant of Venice
Production-slant: The clash of different attitudes to living.
The sharp contrast in the setting of the two opening scenes would emerge in the producer's handling of the reading. The group is then set on the alert for the emergence of life-styles in the way the play grows, in *where* action takes place. They think about such matters as setting as a clue to the things people mind about: the only homes entered, distinctive features of these—Portia and Belmont, Shylock and his house. Off-stage places. Changing places—Venice to Belmont, Belmont to Venice. Setting for the Shylock-Portia conflict. Setting of the final sequence.

Julius Caesar
Production-slant: Makers of History—"The knot of us be called/The men that gave their country liberty".
Given lively production work, pupils can hardly help noticing how personal names resound in the opening scenes, how individuals are isolated from the shifting crowds by the device. They are set to hear for themselves how the naming technique is played with throughout the action: self-naming; how frequently interlocutors use one another's names; lists of names 'pricked' for death; Caesar's naming of the conspirators (II. ii), Antony's repeating the gesture (III, i); Antony's use of Brutus's name (V. iv); the persistence of Caesar's name. Such noticing should lead to recognition of how all this draws us to question the role of the individual in great events, and of the central importance of Caesar's ambition for the 'name' of king.

Romeo and Juliet
Production-slant: Imprisonment of life in chance.
A problem with this play is how to help young readers to be open to the poetic richness, an openness essential to their being able to go beneath the surface story. One way is to set them listening to certain distinctive signals in the poetry. An important recurrent signal is the image of enclosure, which begins early in the play and steadily increases till all action is 'entombed'. Start them off by showing them how Romeo is first spoken of: "stole into the covert", "in his chamber pens himself", "so secret and so close". From that they watch the accumulation of walled places, confined places, barriers to freedom, windows; the friar's cell,

Mercutio's truckle-bed, the apothecary's shop; Romeo's calling Juliet a shrine, Juliet's "poor prisoner in his twisted gyves"; how the images of tomb and grave occur long before Juliet's evocation of the place of death; Juliet's looking down on Romeo's whitened face; Juliet's bed "within the curtains"—all leading inexorably to the final imprisonment. The effort to hear certain patterns in the language heightens attentiveness and facilitates realization of meaning as concrete. Such attentiveness to detail is the beginning of a grasp of 'the essential difference between "guilty creatures sitting at a play" and those sitting at a sermon', some recognition of the essence of dramatic art which takes 'only a few fragmentary details, mere hints and indications of the vast movements, currents and powers, of the infinite variety that lies below'**(18)**. At this stage, we cannot discourse on the nature of dramatic art, but we can help the pupils to be open to the signals they are capable of picking up.

It is important that whatever specific noticing is looked for should be related to the way the producer is handling the play. There are other levels of recognition at which one might aim, depending on the production-slant. A competent class would be able to follow the relationship between theme and action, for instance. Say that the production-slant chosen for *The Merchant of Venice* were 'a world of lenders and borrowers'. Attention would be focused on how money affects the action of the play, determines behaviour, starts up conflicts, colours relationships and so on. Pupils would watch for how much everyone talks about getting and spending, how the subject dominates private concerns. Even the lovers' moonlight and music are borrowed; Lorenzo's stars are "patines of bright gold".

If the production-slant of *Julius Caesar* were 'manipulation', the level of response opened might again be that of the relationship between theme and action. The emphasis of attention would be on what moves a character to a particular course of action; on how much individual decision is influenced by other people; on techniques of persuasion, not only in the great manipulation scene when Antony makes the mob his instrument, but from the very beginning, where Marullus and Flavius persuade the crowd to disperse, right through to Brutus's persuading Strato to hold the sword while he runs on it.

Or say that the production-slant chosen for *Romeo and Juliet* were the intense isolation of the lovers in the world of everyday. Collaboration during the reading might be directed towards the sheer concrete reality of the world within which the private transforming experience happens. Production would aim at enabling the group to discover the richness of sense experience, the ceaseless response of flesh and blood, which so weights the play. It is out of a background of "dull earth" that the lovers' story, transformed by union or by separation, is isolated. Set the group to watch for the signals of common experience: the hot, restless streets, the gentle air of surrounding woods; the noise of work; the discomfort of ordinary aches and pains; the 'scratch' of a death-wound; overcrowded rooms and private rooms; late-night revellers in empty streets; the taste of wormwood; the smell of cooking; the squalor of a plague-silent street; a rope-ladder and the shock of violent news; mockery and laughter, groans and tears, the cold of fear. A good point at which to start the pupils on this kind of noticing is I. iv. The extravagance of the Queen Mab speech is less puzzling if the sleepers are seen as concretely as the verse directs, with their twitching knees, fingers, noses, lips, ears.

The focusing of attention on certain specific 'hints and indications of vast movements' does not exclude noticing other hints. Indeed, the purpose of specific attention is to heighten attentiveness, to cause concentration. Everything the producer does aims at stimulating the group to bring a real consciousness to the play they are reading. He is all the time aware of how the thing is working, ready to take direction from actual response, to seize the opportunity to open new levels.

The Comedies: first reading

"If this were played upon a stage now, I could condemn it as an improbable fiction" (*Twelfth Night*). Fabian's comment strikes a central teaching problem—how to forestall condemnation of 'the deliberate unreality of the comedies'**(19)**. Even Shakespeare has little chance against the severity of the judgement, 'That's stupid,' once it has been pronounced. It is one reason why the comedies are not plays to start with—apart from *The Merchant of Venice* where the realistic force of the non-comic element diverts attention from the unreality. Young readers need to have some familiarity with dramatic conventions, need to connect Shakespeare with enjoyment if the classroom is to accommodate the exquisite make-believe of *As You Like It*, the blend of rapture, hilarity, anger of *Twelfth Night*. Further, for the inexperienced reader, there is the stumbling-block of the verbal wit of another age, the Elizabethan delight in language constantly doubling back on itself.

This calls for imaginative preparation on the part of the teacher/producer. Success in the play-reading stage is vital. The reading planned needs to aim at catching something of the lightness of speed which the comedies have on the stage; the production-slant needs to match the particular comedy; the enterprise needs to reflect the teacher's own pleasure in nonsense and irreverence.

As has often been said, each comedy creates its own distinctive mode. Common to all is enjoyment of life, but each has its own centre of hilarity; common to all is the game of love, but each has its own way of playing the game; common to all is delight in intricate pattern, but the patterns are different. There are just two points to be made about the classroom approach to any comedy. The first is that the producer should take the class into his confidence straightaway—deliberately expose the fact of the unreality and explain how he 'sees' the game. The second is that the production-slant should focus on situation and pattern, not on verbal wit. In the first reading, that wit is best let run with the minimum of explanation, let seem nonsense, even if strictly it isn't. Shakespeare does after all use nonsense some of the time, which is warrant enough, and speed of exchange may cause laughter where painstaking explanation will stop it.

As You Like It

Introductory comment: In the first shot at Shakespeare, introductory comment aimed at stimulating the children to imagine a more or less realistic setting, to visualize actual places. At this level, if *As You Like It* is not their first taste of Shakespeare, a more strictly theatrical setting is possible. The producer, in his introduction, evokes a *stage* setting, collaborates with the unreality by describing how he would translate it into visual terms. The 'translation' that I have used for this play is that of a complicated game in which the bright pieces are in continuous movement. The purpose of the game is to see how many new combinations can be made with the pieces. 'The pattern of *As You Like It* comes not from a mere repetition of steps, but from constant little shifts and changes' **(20)**. The game-image is a way of bringing that pattern to life; the group is caught up in discovering the various moves, challenged from the beginning to keep up with Shakespeare's skill in manipulating the several pieces.

The following is an indication of the kind of thing the producer draws attention to.

Act I: Selection of pieces from the fairy-tale. Tentative first moves which suggest that Shakespeare hasn't quite decided what game to play with them. For example, Rosalind changes size in the course of the act; Duke Frederick loves his niece in scene i; he can't stand the sight of her in scene iii. The play begins unwittily with a catalogue of injustice. ('Tedious' is a frequent word throughout the play.) The gloom seems to be about to continue in scene ii until the sudden turnabout of Rosalind's mood. This is the first shift of the pieces—Rosalind, unlike Orlando, "can forget the condition of her estate" and laugh at it. Other moves follow. The two unfortunates are brought together and properly fall in love. Celia remains an odd piece. Shakespeare decides to move the whole game away from the court.

When the first act has been read, there is a pause to examine the elements of the game. Plainly, a love-story has started. Certain data are established: that it is "possible on such a sudden" to fall in love; that the plots of the wicked are foiled; that the good can escape from "this working-day world" to a "golden world". Shakespeare is inviting his audience to join in the game, to escape from the "briars" of everyday life into "holiday foolery". The fact that the improbable is a deliberate part of the game is made clear; disguise, for instance, is to be taken as impenetrable. The stage-pattern is examined. It seldom takes more than a hint for pupils to see for themselves that the dominant pattern is the duologue.

Act II: The forest setting takes over. In a production which is emphasizing the unreality, my Arden is a stage-forest, a matter of painted hangings inspired by the tapestry quality of the scene-painting passages. If one is working with a bright class, it is possible to invite their collaboration in artifice straightaway. How might the Duke's opening speech be translated into a stage set? What is the joke in his dismissing the court as "painted pomp"? With inexperienced classes it may be wise to treat setting naturalistically.

The game continues. A "desert inaccessible" is full of characters. The "little shifts and changes" are before us in Arden also. The Duke, like his daughter, "translates the stubbornness of fortune". His contented sermon on the simple life is punctuated by Jaques's rebuke, but the rebuke in turn is punctured by the fact that Jaques is preaching to wild deer. In the forest too, the pieces show a tendency to move in pairs. Figures change partners and each change is a change in the angle of seeing. Youth and age serve one another (Orlando/Adam). Youth dismisses the ignorance of age (Corin/Silvius). Love groans and love mocks (Silvius/Corin). The forest is "free from peril" but not from the plain need for food and shelter. A song begins in praise of the simple life and ends in mockery of it. The churlish Frederick is matched by a churlish farmer. A "libertine" offers to clean the wicked world. A young man's courage is met by mockery. A professional philosopher catalogues the ages of life and not one of them is represented on the stage, unless it be the philosopher himself—"full of wise saws". The same philosopher meets a professional fool and hasn't the wit to see that he is outfooled. A song is sung about man's ingratitude while the stage shows an example of the truest gratitude.

Acts III and IV: The centre of this comedy is a delightful twist of dramatic convention—for nothing happens. The only gestures to plot are tidied away at the beginning and end of the sequence: Oliver's departure and the convenient miracle of his arrival. In between, with "holiday humour", the pattern shifts and changes like a kaleidoscope. There is a new rule: only lovers are allowed to speak at this stage of the game. So the sour non-lover Jaques is pushed out of play when he tries to take part, but not the kindly Corin who loved in his day.

Rosalind is the unifying energy of the forest game and the producer's chorus-work stresses her exuberant enjoyment, in order to carry young readers through the "curvetting" wit. It is important to keep alive the fact that she is *wooing* Orlando, that she is "fathoms deep in love". Her impatient ardour inspires her to create a game within a game, and thus give the whole game a new twist when she intervenes in the Silvius/Phebe affair. The active collaboration of the readers is constantly invited. How many faces and voices has love? Who comes out best in the various encounters? Who works the harder—teacher/Rosalind or pupil/Orlando? What is Touchstone up to with his repetition of Audrey's name? What is Celia's part in the game? Why is it Celia and not Rosalind who dominates the meeting with Oliver? What on earth has happened to Oliver anyway? What moves does Rosalind's disguise make possible? And what is the point of the dressing-up of the Duke, his court, and Orlando?

Act V: That the game is nearing its end is marked by a new complication—William, briskly disposed of. It is the moment when Touchstone's being the touchstone is most amusingly displayed, for this complication comes before the riddling of the quartet so that, by a nice piece of comic inversion, the major is made to seem an echo of the minor. The joke is taken further in the size of Touchstone's role in this act: he starts up the music which accompanies the final move of the lovers to their proper places; he leads off the coupling; he has the cleverest solo performance in the last tongue-in-cheek mockery of Jaques.

The entry of Jaques de Boys can be presented as Shakespeare's way of breaking up the game by pushing it as far as it will go; it is a hilarious threat that the game could go on for ever. The outrageous improbability counters the acid of Jaques's separation at the end. The final joke is perhaps that Jaques goes on with the game, takes on a new role, while the healthily cheerful people go on with living.

Twelfth Night

Twelfth Night is "a very opal", a play of such subtle variety and openness of meaning as to be a producer's joy. High romance and blind folly, explosive feeling and equally explosive buffoonery, rapid, intricate action, characters who can be variously interpreted—the blend makes it necessary for the teacher/producer to be very clear about his production. The first reading has two main aims: to help readers to enjoy the craft which can keep several balls whirling in the air at a moment; to let loose in the classroom characters of immense vitality. In the introductory comment, convention is given its full value: the class is invited to a party 'full of games, revels, tricks and disguises'(**21**). While there is no need to raise the problem of whether the play was written for a Twelfth Night celebration, some information about Twelfth Night customs wakens expectation of amusement. It is a play in which Shakespeare, in a specially vigorous way, makes the collaboration of the audience part of the enterprise. A great deal of the entertainment springs from who knows what at any given moment(**22**). The audience almost always knows everything. This feature suggests a way of causing involvement—the game of "What dost thou know?". The privileged position of the audience is explained. The challenge throughout will be to answer the Duke's question. What is the state of knowledge of characters and audience in the various complications? The game can be played orally. Findings might be graphically recorded on a chart with three circles representing Ignorance, Partial Knowledge, Full Knowledge. Coloured flags represent the characters. The satisfaction of being able to demonstrate superior knowledge gives young readers an invaluable sense of mastery.

The "What dost thou know?" game takes in without strain the interlocking of the plot elements, the crossing-over of the main story and the below-stairs jesting; the way finally the separate parts of the 'catch' are brought safely home. To ensure that the vitality of the characters is communicated needs alert preparation for the day's reading. The thing to keep in mind is that the vitality has its source in the interaction of the characters rather than in individual action. Viola's trusting response to the Captain at the beginning establishes contact as the mode for the whole story. Characters cannot leave one another alone. They find themselves in their immense capacity for affecting and being affected by their company. Even Malvolio's obsessive self-love cannot stand up against the "giddy activity" round him. The sole exception is Feste, and a large part of the impact of this Fool is that he is the only untouchable character.

Example of preparation: First meeting of Viola and Olivia (I. v). Expectations raised by Malvolio's description of Viola at the gate. Hasty entry of Viola, masking nervousness under direct approach. Sharp-voiced—"shrewishly". Launches straight into message. Quick reaction to giggling—"saucy". Calls audience on to her side—"I am not that I play". Olivia provocative. V. attacks—"You do usurp yourself . . .". O. stung to counter-attack—"It is more like to be feigned". Smart cutting Maria down to size. Sudden change of tone: V. no longer "rude"—"It alone concerns your ear . . .". O. curious, impressed. V. and O. alone—deadlock of first exchanges. Unveiling breaks deadlock. Contrast between V.'s urgency, O's mockery. O. yields. Masks slip in willow-cabin speech—V. rapt, O. puzzled, fascinated. *N.B.* O. falling in love. O. disconcerted—uncertainty of "Get you to your lord . . .". V.'s refusal of money—very much the victor. Aware of change in O.?

The comic scenes need to be taken fast. Jokes requiring explication are best cut. Exaggeration rather than subtlety guides the presentation of Sir Toby's preposterous self-indulgence, Sir Andrew's imbecility, Malvolio's conceit. Each needs a recognizable trick of the voice. As Feste says, "You must allow *vox*". The class decides on a particular way of speaking for each. The Kitchen scene, the duel, the Sir Topas scene, seldom cause difficulties, but the Box-tree scene can sag. To get it off the page successfully, the teacher/producer takes on the role of a fourth eye-witness, whose commentary makes visible the behaviour of the others: the appearance and disappearance of Sir Toby's bulk, of Sir Andrew's long face;

the tic of Malvolio's posturing; the distinctive noises the spies make. The letter-reading sequence needs plenty of business. Pick up the directions in Malvolio's commentary—"baffle Sir Toby", "wash off", "point-device", "commend my yellow stockings", "strange", "stout", "smiling". It has worked well on a number of occasions to give Malvolio from the beginning of the play the oddity of a slight time-lag between word and action—the affected gesture coming always just out of time with the word.

One of the marvels of *Twelfth Night* is the art by which the all-knowing audience is given the thrill of surprise. This is not something that can be explained to young readers, but chorus-work should ensure that the moments of surprise are not missed—the sudden flash of emotion, the unforeseen meeting, the unexpected element in the expected event. For example: Viola's revelation that she loves Orsino, her pretence that she gave Olivia a ring; the tale of Cesario's sister; Malvolio's fantasy that he left Olivia sleeping; Sir Andrew's being a witness to Olivia's love-play with Cesario; the meeting of Antonio and Viola; Sebastian accepting Olivia's proposal; Orsino's threat to kill Cesario. It is the cumulative effect of such moments which prepares for the wonder of the meeting of Viola and Sebastian. I should pause before Sebastian's entry to get the class to visualize the stage. There are several people present—Viola, Orsino and his lords; Olivia, her attendants, and a priest; Antonio and the officers. Sir Toby and his friends have just made their noisy exit and everyone is still watching that. At Sebastian's entry all on the stage freeze into position. From that moment until Viola says "I am Viola", only Sebastian moves. The recognition dialogue is spoken against absolute stillness. The difference between Viola's delighted understanding of what is happening and Sebastian's gradually coming to understanding is brought out by the way each speaks—Viola's quietness, Sebastian's urgency.

The Tragedies

The great tragedies are the supreme examples of the several ways in to Shakespeare. The challenge is to serve Shakespeare honestly, to guide new readers into a huge world without reducing its scale or losing them at the frontier. At whatever level we are taking on the challenge, the thing to trust is the intensity of experience that Shakespeare's art makes available to all sorts of audiences. Only a non-dramatic reading can blur the impact. What follows is a description of how the first reading of *Macbeth* may be conducted at different levels.

Macbeth: a first shot reading

I have two kinds of audience in mind here: pupils who meet Shakespeare for the first time as part of a prescribed course and early school-leavers in their final year to whom the teacher wants to give the chance of enjoying at least one of the plays. *Macbeth* is an ideal choice in the latter situation. The plot moves rapidly, the moral issue is clear and of universal relevance; the splendours of the poetry carry readers over lexical difficulties.

Production takes advantage of the high degree of suspense in the plot. The response of readers ignorant of the play makes one aware of how Shakespeare holds his audience in intense question. Up to the murder of Duncan the questions are 'who?' and 'when?'. After the murder suspense shifts to the risk of exposure and retribution and to the unpredictability of Macbeth.

The play can be taken at speed even with completely inexperienced readers. It is helpful to think in terms of three parts rather than five acts. *Part 1* The King-killer: Acts I and II. *Part 2* The Tyrant: Acts III and IV. *Part 3* Tied to the stake: Act V. Although the play is relatively short, some abridgement is necessary. Cuts are suggested in the outline below. In my experience, the amount of chorus-work needed in a first-shot reading diminishes more quickly with this play than with any other. Once the first act is over, it is frequently surprising how little appears to be necessary. Again, *Macbeth* provokes more frequent spontaneous interruption from the audience than is usual, a sign that the play is communicating at a deeper level than is explicitly aimed at in the production-slant. One example from a group of low ability range will be useful. At Macbeth's speech, "Had I but died one hour before this chance", one member interrupted, 'That's a lie'. Another countered at once, 'No, it isn't. He wants to be back before the murder'.

Introductory comment is brief, concentrated simply on evoking the places of the action—a grim, bleak landscape, huge torch-lit castles whose corridors disappear into the shadows. Throughout, scene-setting is vital, not only to stir the imagination for the day's reading, but to bring into the classroom something of the powerful dramatic effect of the scene sequence: the quickly changing setting of the four opening scenes; the plunge into darkness with the Letter scene, a darkness which, apart from the brief sunset of Duncan's arrival, is sustained until the England scene; the alternation of closed castle and open country in Act V.

Part 1: The King-killer

It is only in the four opening scenes that new readers may be confused about what is happening. It is wise to make sure that they are clear about the prophecies, Duncan's naming Malcolm as his heir, and his decision to visit Macbeth's castle.

It works well to present the witches as faceless shadows, who speak in a high, unnatural chant. (Banquo's description, I. iii, can be cut.) Give the three sisters an attendant coven from the beginning and let the whole coven join in at any part marked *All*. Read scene i twice to establish a mode for these characters.

Scene ii can be cut. The producer supplies the facts: King Duncan and his sons, war in Scotland, treachery of Thane of Cawdor. Colour the narrative by emphasis on the noise of battle and the heroic fury of Macbeth and Banquo.

Macbeth's first soliloquy, "Two truths are told", needs producer glossing before it is read: his uncertainty about whether the prophecies are good or bad, his fear and excitement. This is the moment for suggesting an image of Macbeth's mind as a castle whose doors are repeatedly opened to the audience. Throughout the play, understanding of the soliloquies is greatly helped if readers see them as moments of entering that castle and following Macbeth through the winding corridors of his imagination. In this first soliloquy the word 'murder' is not revealed in the producer's preliminary comment, but come upon suddenly in the reading. The "If it were done" soliloquy is a good point for reinforcing the notion of a concrete following of Macbeth's thought: each surprising step is presented as entry into yet another secret place. Generally, this soliloquy is best read by the producer.

Lady Macbeth's first appearance should come as a surprise. Stress the intensity of her excitement at the vision of the "golden round". It stirs imagination if the ecstasy of the invocation of the spirits is linked with witchcraft**(23)**. Bring out the suspense of the meeting between Macbeth and Lady Macbeth, the contrast between his brief words and her eloquence.

If possible, the murder sequence should be read in one session. At least scenes ii and iii should not be split. It is worth preparing the group for the mode of scene ii. Explain that the audience sees two things throughout: what is visible on the stage and what the two characters in turn watch in imagination. First there is Lady Macbeth's imagining of what is happening in Duncan's room, and then Macbeth's appalled exploration of the new chamber in the castle of his thought. Give directions to the readers—to Lady Macbeth that she is intensely aware of the danger of discovery, to Macbeth that he is aware of nothing but the horror of his deed. Then let the scene run without interruption. Provide the knocking.

The producer had best take the Porter's part himself, making it grim comedy. Work up expectation for Macbeth's entry. Remind Macduff that he has a whole castle to rouse.

The choric scenes are producer narrative only. The elements to convey in III. iv are the beginning of "hours dreadful and things strange" in Scotland, Macduff's suspicion, Macbeth's crowning.

Part 2: The tyrant

The focus in this part is on Macbeth's bloody progress, "the taste of fears", the widening gulf between husband and wife.

To help the group to hear the doubleness of the dialogue with Banquo (III. i), tell them to listen for hints of a secret line of thought under the royal manner: "Ride you this afternoon? ... Is't far you ride? ... Fail not our feast! ... Till you return at night ... Goes Fleance with you?" The dialogue with the murderers can be abridged. Suggested cuts are 79–84, 98–108, 121–126.

The climactic III. ii is another scene to be read without interruption. If the poetry does not work, paraphrase certainly will not. Prepare for the reading by reminding the group that this is the first time we have seen the two alone since the murder, then let the poetry reveal the airless prison they inhabit now. It is important that Macbeth's part should be taken by one of the better readers.

In a school production, the murder of Banquo was played as sound only—a blacked-out, empty stage, flickering torch-light, voices and sound-effects coming from the wings. This deed-by-night approach is effective in a play-reading also.

Chorus-work for the Banquet scene aims at keeping dramatic excitement high. Stress the festive setting, the splendid garments of the crowned king and queen. Bring out the contrast between Macbeth's uncontrollable terror and Lady Macbeth's efforts to impose a normal surface. Let Banquo's ghost appear each time at Macbeth's call. The exit of the guests marks a drop to the isolation of the royal pair: the tyrant king with his legion of spies and his thirst for power, the exhausted queen. Against this set the new suspense of Macduff's absence.

The Hecate scene can be cut. For the choric scene, III. vi, the producer evokes a country under a reign of terror.

Assemble the whole coven for the Apparition scene. Try using three small groups for the weird sisters and single voices only for the apparitions. Present the murder of Lady Macduff and her children as a hideous sample of the reign of terror, emphasizing the contrast between the domesticity of the setting and the brutality of the murderers.

The first half of the England scene up to the entry of Ross can be replaced by producer narrative. Emphasis is on Malcolm's authority and foresight, his fitness to be king. The pathos of the second half is prepared for by stressing Macduff's unawareness of what has happened at home.

Part 3: Tied to the stake

The Sleepwalking scene needs no comment apart from the preliminary evocation of night and silence. Give the text to the three readers to think about before the reading.

The remainder of the play should be read in one period. Evoke the image of an avenging army closing in relentlessly on Macbeth and the narrowing of his power. Bring out the suspense of his violent swings of mood.

Reading *Macbeth* with an experienced class

'Each tragedy has its own unmistakable individual nature, its own colour; it has its own landscape, its own atmosphere, its own diction'(**24**). At any point, this distinctive life of the play is visible. A way of choosing an approach for one of the tragedies is to open the play at random and let what is found in the two pages inspire a production-slant. Opening *Macbeth* three times yielded the following extracts:

1) From "Your Majesty loads our house" I. vi to "Why have you left the chamber?" I. vii.

2) From "What is this,/That rises like the issue of a king?" to "Come in, without there." IV. i.

3) From "The multitudinous seas" II. ii to "it makes him and it mars" II. iii.

Examination of the three extracts reveals the unity of *Macbeth*. In all there is the charged atmosphere of the play; major themes and images are heard. The stage-picture in each reinforces Macbeth's separation from his fellow men, not only in the real soliloquy of the first and the virtual soliloquy of the third, but in his absence from the welcome to Duncan and the call, "Come in, without there". At the same time, to set the three together reveals the variety of the play.

1) Production-slant: "To find the mind's construction".
The characteristic intensity of the soliloquy suggests a production-slant which focuses attention on the inner drama, the creation of another world beyond the apparent world of the action. The emphasis is on how we live in Macbeth himself, how freely we share in his experience, how much he makes us see beyond the immediate event. Our knowledge begins on his first appearance: the dramatic surprise of access to the warrior's inner world in "Two truths are told". Producer comment stresses the importance of the first rapt withdrawal as a guide to how the play works. From then on, the reading tries to explore the nature of that inner world. One result of this exploration is an understanding of how Shakespeare holds our sympathy for Macbeth.

This approach is most rewarding with pupils who are already open to the language of poetry. What one encourages above all is *listening* to Macbeth as a way of following him into the depths. After the Murder scene has been read, another aspect of his 'raptness' can be suggested: how seldom Macbeth engages in real dialogue, how frequently we are aware of his inner world even when he appears to turn towards the outer world. Eventually, the withdrawal becomes the literal trap of Dunsinane. There would be no producer-intervention at all at those moments when Macbeth's imagination ranges furthest—the soliloquies, the Murder scene, and III. ii.

The aspect of dramatic technique which matches this production-slant is how Shakespeare's art counters the risk of our being sucked helplessly into Macbeth's imagination. The key is there in the starting extract. On one level it is the moral weight of Duncan's innocence; on another it is Lady Macbeth's practicality. The choric scenes are produced as providing a necessary balance, a view of Macbeth from outside. In the last act these 'side-line' scenes move toward the centre of the stage; the chorus figures become active participants in the overthrow of Macbeth.

2) Production-slant: "Night's predominance".
The production-slant this extract suggests is the struggle between the forces of good and evil. The action is watched as the drama of what happens when evil is released by one man's failure in moral responsibility, the spreading poison of the murder of the king. From the beginning, the producer alerts the readers to the powerful suggestions of unnaturalness. The witches are "instruments of darkness", "night's black agents", seeking to invade and destroy "good things of day". The "foul and fair" link between the witches and Macbeth points straight to the source of danger. Macbeth's real responsibility is made clear. Scene ii shows him "in the day of success", guardian of the state against evil. The "two truths are told" reflection shows him to be aware that what is in question is the choice between good and evil. The thought of murder makes his "seated heart knock at his ribs,/Against the use of nature". Up to the murder of Duncan, producer emphasis is on the suspense of the struggle between the two forces *within* the "single state of man". The dagger speech shows Macbeth's awareness of the universal significance of the outcome. After the murder, the struggle shifts to the whole state. The knocking and the clangour of the alarm bell are heard as immediate revolt against the evil deed. The readers are set to watch the stage as a battleground. On the one hand, to notice the "multiplying villainies" which suggest the apparent triumph of evil: distorted nature, deeds of terror, fears, deceptions, madness, the torn body of the state, the helplessness of natural virtue. On the other, to notice the signs of the survival of good: the Old Man's "benison", the escape of Malcolm, Donalbain, Fleance, Banquo's prayer for peace, the Macduff child's courage, Macduff's integrity. Producer comment prompts recognition of the counterpointing of the Banquet scene and the England scene: in the first the signs of decay in Macbeth's isolated and frenzied kingplaying; in the second the signs of new growth in the gathering of good men about Malcolm's kingliness.

On the level of dramatic technique, scene sequence would be important in this approach. An advanced class might also be alerted to the subtlety with which the conflict between good and evil is constantly present in the language. For instance, the moment when the torment of evil is most vividly illuminated—III. ii—is also the moment when we hear the most tender image of Duncan's death.

3) Production-slant: "Rancours in the vessel of my peace".
Macbeth's cry "Wake Duncan with thy knocking! I would thou couldst", suggests a production-slant where the emphasis is on the effect of evil on

the evil-doer himself. The line of attention would be the descent of Macbeth and Lady Macbeth into a hell of their own making. The reading would focus on the journey from freedom of choice to the slavery of compulsion. The readers would be set to discover each stage in the transformation of the heroic warrior into the "dead butcher". In the first act, producer comment would aim at bringing out the potential for good in Macbeth: his truly deserved high reputation, his friendship with Banquo, his moral horror at the surfacing of "black and deep desires", his absence from the welcome to Duncan. The "If it were done" soliloquy would be read as a victory over the temptation of ambition; progress from the argument of fear of personal consequences to the arguments of morality and compassion. It would be left to the pupils to decide just why he is then so quickly out-argued by Lady Macbeth. That evil is already beginning its destructive work within Macbeth becomes visible in the dagger speech. In the Murder scene itself, he cannot shut his eyes against the irreversible change in his being. From then on, the readers watch the tragic distortion of his natural gifts: how easy lying and murder become; the lack of compunction in Banquo's murder; the wantonness of the murder of Macduff's wife and children; the suspicions, the fears, the uncontrollable anger. It is necessary to guard against the exploration of personal evil being conducted in the spirit of the examining magistrate. A very important element would be Macbeth's capacity for suffering. This attends him all the way from the vision of eternal sleeplessness to the negation of life itself.

Attention to Lady Macbeth again brings out the fact that evil destroys natural gifts. The first half of the play shows that commitment to evil has already perverted her qualities of courage, single-mindedness, loyalty to her husband, practical resourcefulness. The seeds of madness are already there in her deliberate suppression of natural feeling. In the Discovery scene, the readers can be set to suggest reasons for the fainting. In the Banquet scene, emphasis is on the pathos of her futile efforts to make all well.

The Banquet scene and the Sleepwalking scene suggest the aspect of dramatic technique which might be stressed in this production-slant. Each scene brings out clearly for young readers the dramatic use of reverberation; in each, Lady Macbeth's behaviour is a distorted reflection of earlier behaviour. In the early part of the play, producer comment will make sure that the beginnings of the echo pattern are not missed; the "fair is foul" repetition, for instance, and the invocation to darkness of both Macbeth and Lady Macbeth. Lady Macbeth's "I feel now/The future in the instant" is a good moment for wakening attention to echoes of gesture and event as well as of words.

We cannot reflect upon a work of art unless we have experienced it imaginatively. That the play should first possess imagination is vital to the later business of thinking about it. The efforts of the teacher/producer during the play-reading are directed to keeping the way clear for the satisfaction of the imagination. What we want to make possible is an active, joyful involvement. Success in this greatly simplifies the task of closer study. Enjoyment gives confidence, a confidence which is carried over to the stage of reflection upon the experience.

4

The pupil as annotator

Whether closer study of the play follows immediately upon the play-reading is a matter of choice. Sometimes pupils are eager to start work on it straightaway; sometimes they elect to turn to other parts of the course and leave the second reading of the play till later. The second reading aims to create close familiarity with the text and to show pupils how to keep a written record of their thinking about it, while at the same time leading them to a deeper level of enjoyment. Note-book work is an essential part of the study. As the reading proceeds, each pupil constructs his own reference book. The work involved strengthens his grasp of the play and causes an invaluable confidence, a readiness to read with the expectation of being able to take independent possession of a work of literature. The note-book is a record of individual attention to the play. What is contained in it represents what the *pupil* can think about Shakespeare. It is not confused by the inappropriate matter that so often clutters commercially produced aids: the dating of the play, for instance, which is irrelevant for the young reader, or scene summaries which he could provide for himself if he needed them. For pupils whose control of literacy is poor, the transcription involved in note-book work gives practice in accuracy; learning to make the layout of a page an instrument of communication develops attention to orderly expression.

Starting note-book work

To begin with, the purpose of keeping a note-book is explained: the usefulness of a personal reference book as a way of coming to grips with the play, as a way of remembering, as a basis for answering questions, as a tool for revision. The book should have a life expectancy of two to three years, so it needs to be sturdy. Clear layout is stressed: at whatever page the book is opened, it should be possible to see what is going on. It is sensible not to be mean about paper: there should be space for later additions.

Basic conventions and layout are demonstrated on the blackboard: how to make clear the distinction between quotation and comment, to embed quotation in comment, to indicate omission, to make significant words stand out. The first tasks set should be straightforward, aimed chiefly at giving practice in selecting and presenting textual evidence. What follows are suggestions for preliminary training in the skill, the kind of work that can start during the first reading.

The Merchant of Venice
Production-slant: 'a world of lenders and borrowers'. Aspect for note-book record: constant references to money.
While Act I is being read, the pupils will be commenting orally on how often money is a topic of conversation. When the act has been read, they set about making a note-book record of their observations. The instructions would run like this: Collect the references to money. Enter them according to the different characters. Use headings to show the attitude to money of each one.

Sample note-book extract:
Act I *Antonio*
Shrewd business-man:

> My ventures are not in one bottom trusted,
> Nor in one place; nor is my whole estate
> Upon the fortune of this present year.
>
> My meaning in saying he is a *good* man, is to have you
> understand me that he is *sufficient*.

Uses money to help his friends:

> My *purse*, my person, my extremest means
> Lie all *unlocked* to your occasions.
>
> Try what my credit can in Venice do.
> That shall be *racked* even to the uttermost
> *To furnish thee* to Belmont . . .

Believes that taking interest on loans is wrong:

> . . . I neither lend nor borrow
> By taking nor by giving of *excess*.
>
> Signor Antonio, many a time and oft
> In the Rialto you have *rated* me
> About my money and my *usances*.

As You Like It:
Aspect for note-book work: the patterning of the game.
Pupils keep a record of the echoes they notice. The producer's handling of the reading makes sure that all see the obvious details in the design. Recognition of more subtle details varies from pupil to pupil, as is shown

in the following entries from the same group. Both pupils are dealing with the opening lines of v. ii.

Excerpt A

Love at first sight: Oliver falls for Celia as suddenly as Rosalind fell for Orlando at the beginning, and Phebe for Rosalind in the middle.

Excerpt B

More *love at first sight:* Orlando's question echoes Celia's at the beginning (I. iii). Now Celia is caught as Rosalind was. There is a difference in the wooing though. Oliver does the wooing of Celia and wins her as quickly as he loves her. Orlando is wooed by Rosalind over several scenes.

The question, "Is't possible?" is a joke of the whole play. Shakespeare keeps it up to the end. The last scene begins, "Dost thou believe?" By that time we believe anything!

Macbeth

Production-slant: The effect of evil on the evil-doer. Aspect for note-book record: The widening gulf between Macbeth and Lady Macbeth.

Excerpt from an entry for I. vii.

Macbeth gives his wife two reasons for going "no further with this business". Duncan has "honoured him of late". He has "bought golden opinions from all sorts of people". It is surprising that he does not give her any of the reasons he thinks of during the soliloquy, but two new ones. The impression made on the audience is that there is already a distance between them.

1 Henry IV: Dramatic Coherence

Keeping a note-book record during the first reading is, I think, essential with *1 Henry IV* and *Richard II.* One of the problems with these plays is helping readers to hold the narrative line clearly in their heads. A way of doing this is to open the level of dramatic coherence and to set the pupils keeping a record of how the shape of the play is reflected in the visible stage-pattern, how the different strands are knit together as the play proceeds. It is a more illuminating way of treating plot than the scene or act summary, and helps pupils to master complications, not as a memory task but as satisfying patterns. For example, in *1 Henry IV* three sources of conflict emerge in the first scene. Internal politics: the unrest of the Northern lords—the Percy conflict with Bolingbroke. External politics: the trouble on the Welsh and Scottish borders—Glendower and Douglas. Domestic relationships: the trouble between the King and Prince Hal. Following the development of these sources of conflict is a way of seeing how the play is shaped, how the three lines converge, cross, play off one another until the final resolution. Note-book work is a record of the growing pattern.

Sample note-book entry for *1 Henry IV* I. iii

Development of internal conflict

The King warns the Northern Lords (Northumberland, Hotspur, Worcester) that he will no longer be patient with their defiance of his authority (1–9). He banishes Worcester from the court for "danger and disobedience" (14–20). He orders Hotspur to yield him the Scottish prisoners without "proviso or exception" (118–120). Hotspur explodes in anger against the "King of Smiles" (237–240), and swears that he will not obey him (123–124; 212–215), that he will give his whole mind to ways of hurting him (226–227). Worcester discloses a plan of rebellion against the king.

Link between internal and external sources of conflict

The King refuses Hotspur's request that he should ransom Mortimer, Hotspur's brother-in-law, who has been taken prisoner by Glendower, the Welsh lord. The King claims that Mortimer is a traitor, who did not fight against Glendower, but joined him willingly (79–91).

Worcester's plan of rebellion includes alliance with the Scottish Douglas and the Welsh Glendower (256–265; 291–294).

Link between internal political conflict and domestic conflict

In his reference to the "sword-and-buckler Prince of Wales", Hotspur mentions the disagreement between the Prince and the King who "loves him not/And would be glad he met with some mischance".

The second reading: the level of characterization

Characterization is an aspect of the plays which is commonly falsified by reducing the characters to bundles of plus and minus personality traits. The method is as unproductive as it is reductive: spotting traits and affixing labels works against the pupils' discovery of the richness of life in Shakespeare's characters. It is also false to the way a dramatic work comes to theatrical existence. Producers and actors do not write character sketches; they discover authentic dramatic identity from building an enactment.

Developing the ability to reflect upon character, to read the multiple signals to inner life, is a gradual affair which can be profitably engaged in only when the class is acquainted with the play. The second reading, it seems to me, is the right moment for making study of character the explicit focus of attention. During the first reading, the pupils do, of course, react to the human behaviour they are watching. They are quick to pass moral judgement, which is naturally marked by the narrowness of their experience and their current personal preoccupations. This is not to say that these first impressions are valueless. They are as important as the impressions of any audience at a performance, and are part of the deeper understanding that comes with later reflection. The second reading is a close-up exploration of what caused these impressions, a testing of their validity. It is important to keep the primary experience alive during later reflection upon it. In this connection, there is one specifically dramatic task worth setting before the second reading—an experiment in production. Small groups of pupils are assigned a certain production problem to solve, a problem of showing character in action: Shylock with Jessica; Portia when Bassanio chooses right; Brutus's soliloquy in the orchard; Cassius offering Antony a share in power; Romeo hearing the news of Juliet's death; Juliet when she realizes that it is Tybalt's, not Romeo's, death that the Nurse is lamenting; the Prince, Hotspur and Falstaff at the moment of Hotspur's death. The production teams would work out detailed instructions for pace and tone of speaking, gesture, posture, movement.

To study Shakespeare's characterization is to observe the subtleties and ambiguities of human interaction, which means learning to read more closely, and to interpret the concrete evidence of speech and action. There are different ways of approaching the study. The particular play being studied inspires the way the work is shaped, and the kind of reflection one tries to stimulate in the pupils. The suggestions which follow all have the aim of increasing reading agility and giving opportunity for independent exercise of the skill to discriminate. The kind of study involved leads to a close knowledge of the play as a whole.

Studying a character in depth: the 'trial' method

To put a major character on trial for his choice of a course of action is a lively and popular way of engaging pupils in close study of character. The method gives scope to the strong inclination of adolescents to pass moral judgement, and at the same time confronts them with the danger of doing so on insufficient grounds. It is an effective way of giving training in interpretation and in assembling textual evidence. The work involves all the pupils in both team-work and individual work. Most important of all, perhaps, it is conducted dramatically; the thinking is eventually enacted.

A good preliminary to the work is watching a video-recording or listening to a sound-recording of the whole play, or best of all, if the opportunity arises, seeing it on the stage. After that, the second reading is a matter of team and individual work. The indictment is decided on. The class is divided into three groups—prosecution, defence, jury. Prosecution and defence groups are made up of a legal team—solicitors and barristers—with a number of witnesses. The composition of the legal team depends on the size of the class; there should be at least two solicitors and two barristers. The witnesses are those characters in the play whose evidence is worth attending to in the context of the indictment.

The jury can be of any uneven number. The foreman of the jury may double as clerk of court. Casting within the groups is best done by the teacher, who assigns roles on the basis of his knowledge of the class. Legal work is best in the hands of abler pupils, since the quantity of work is heaviest here. Counsel need to be extrovert and quick-witted; solicitors to be thoughtful and painstaking. Witnesses need to like acting. For reasons of peace and profitability, the teacher plays the part of the judge.

Before the groups separate to prepare for the trial, the rules of evidence are established and the whole class is taught how to assemble and interpret evidence and how to prepare an examination. Only evidence actually *in* the play is admissible. Evidence may not be drawn from other sources, from history, for instance. But hearsay evidence, second-hand evidence, is allowed as long as it is in the text. The whole team is responsible for collecting evidence—solicitors, counsel, witnesses. A witness makes himself thoroughly familiar with the role of the character he is playing. He does not study his part in isolation but in context; he must know why and when he said something as well as what he said. Where evidence involves dialogue between members of the same team, they work on this together. (The importance of a character's function in the play becomes clear in the number of times he works with other characters.) Witnesses discuss their evidence with solicitors and make suggestions as to how it might be used. They try to foresee the unexpected in cross-examination. Solicitors are responsible for organizing evidence, and counsel for deciding what to use and for what purpose. The legal team has the heaviest load, since they need close knowledge of all the possible evidence. They must be able to depend upon thorough support from their witnesses.

The trial of Marcus Brutus

Julius Caesar is a play which lends itself to this method of approaching character. A close study of Brutus's character brings out very clearly the interdependence of the four main characters, and demonstrates that in this play Shakespeare is searching for a hero rather than starting with one. One interesting thing about this particular trial is that one can never predict the outcome; in my experience Brutus's choice of action has been condemned as often as it has been found to be justified.

Preliminary demonstration of assembling and interpreting evidence

A short scene is examined orally; annotation is recorded on the blackboard. For example: Act I Scene iii—The Storm Scene

1–71 Factual evidence: strange events on eve of Ides.

Casca's state of mind:
"breathless" ... "why *stare* you so?"
"It is the part of man to fear and tremble."
"You are *dull*."
Cassius' exhilaration:
"walked about the streets ... unbraced" etc. claims to know "the true cause", reads omens as a clear sign of danger from Caesar.
Case use—Prosecution:
1) Discredit Casca as witness—timid, dull of "blunt fellow" (I. ii)
2) Discredit Cassius as witness—arrogance: claims to know the "true cause".
3) Answer to charge that Caesar was superstitious.
Case use—Defence:
Cassius and Casca men with proper reverence for the part the gods play in affairs of men.
72–120 Factual evidence: "The senators mean to establish Caesar as their king."
Cassius' justification of conspiracy:
Caesar "prodigious grown and fearful", "tyrant", "wolf", "lion" who will destroy Romans.
Case use—Prosecution:
1) Real motive envy: "a man no mightier than ... me", "Poor man!", "so vile a thing as Caesar". cf I. ii.
2) Arrogance: Cassius despises the people of Rome—"trash", "rubbish", "offal".
Case use—Defence:
1) Cassius' conviction of rightness of cause: "an enterprise of honourable-dangerous consequence"; indifference to personal safety: "I know where I will wear this dagger then"; ready to sacrifice himself for Rome.
2) Against charge of arrogance: belief in help of gods who "make the weak more strong".
120–164 Factual evidence: meeting (121–126); affair of letters (142–147)
Case use—Prosecution:
1) Coldblooded planning. Cassius' deceitfulness.
2) Conspirators' awareness of evil of plan: "would appear *offence* in us"—need mask of virtue.
Case use—Defence:
1) Involvement of "noblest-minded Romans".
2) Cassius not ashamed of letters—gives them to others.
3) Use only as evidence of Brutus's ignorance of conspiracy, of source of letters. No deceit in his actions. "He sits high in all the people's hearts."

Note-book work is an extremely important part of the method. The interest of the task, the promise of the trial itself, the individual responsibility, make it easy to demand and get good note-keeping. It is an opportunity for demonstrating how note-book work is related to purpose. Each group is taught separately how to use the appropriate format.

Witnesses
Example: Cassius' annotation of above scene.
Fact:
Storm—evidence of warning from gods. Challenge, not terror. (N.B. 45–52; 68–71)
Motive:
Approval of gods (cf above; N.B. 91–92). Caesar an ordinary man making himself a prodigy. Effect on Rome (103–111). N.B. Casca: "The senators mean to establish Caesar as their king" etc.
N.B. 89–100—importance of liberty to a true Roman. Perhaps quote some of this in court.
Points prosecution may attack:
1) Envy (76; 111). Arrogance (108–9).
2) Affair of letters.
Answer: urgency of cause. Others appealed directly to me to win Brutus, e.g. Cinna: "Cassius, if you could . . ." (140–141).

Solicitors
Solicitors use a scene by scene system of annotation. The emphasis differs for each side, prosecution or defence, but each will note the use the other side might make of the evidence. At the head of each entry there will be a clear indication of context. At the end of each entry there will be an indication of the relative importance of the scene as evidence, and cross-reference to other scenes containing related evidence.
Example: Prosecution entry for I. iii.
Meeting of Cicero, Casca, Cassius, Cinna in storm—eve of Ides of March.
Annotation and case use (prosecution) as in preliminary demonstration above.
Importance: clear evidence of conspiracy. Useful for discrediting Cassius—dishonest and envious, also arrogant. But shows Brutus as not party to conspiracy at this point. For discrediting Cassius see also Brutus/Cassius dialogue (I. ii); meeting of conspirators in Brutus's house (II. i); quarrel between Brutus and Cassius (IV. iii).

Counsel
Counsel organize note-books according to individual characters, building up a file on each under headings which indicate the possible shape of an examination, and bring together evidence from different parts of the play. They are in frequent consultation with solicitors.
Example: Defence counsel file on Casca.

Fact

N.B. I. ii Account of crown offering. Cross-examine Citizen to confirm.

N.B. III. i Assassination. First to strike. cf *Motive* below.

I. iii "Senators mean to establish Caesar as king".

II. i Meeting at Brutus's house

Credibility as witness

I. iii Account of storm. Question on attitude to omens.

N.B. Belief in Roman liberty: willing to choose death.

I. ii "Blunt fellow"—Cassius' answer.

Problem:

I. ii tone of account of crowning; e.g. attitude to Caesar and plebs. Leave for re-examination?

Motive of conspirators

I. iii State of Rome: opinion of Cassius' description—"all these griefs".

Danger of Caesar: (I. ii) Crown offering—Caesar's demeanour, manner of "putting by of crown". "To my thinking, he was very loath to lay his fingers off it."

Relationship with main characters

Brutus: Respect (I. iii): "sits high in people's hearts".

Cassius: Meeting in storm (I. iii). Question on Cassius' behaviour and explanation of omens: Cassius' courage and idealism.

Jury

While the different sides are preparing for the trial, the jury members are also examining the play, working as a group. They may decide to divide responsibility for different sections of the action, or for different characters. They will use the format described in the preliminary demonstration above, and will record questions raised by jury members. For example, a question for the above scene would be the difference between Casca as he appears there and in I. ii. During the trial proper, the jury is entitled to put questions to witnesses through the judge where they feel a point is not sufficiently clear.

Guidelines for examining a witness need to be given to counsel. A basic line is: 1) Establishing credibility of witnesses. 2) Factual evidence. Avoid unnecessary repetition. (The jury is encouraged to stop an examination if there is unnecessary repetition.) 3) Particular points of evidence proper to a given witness. Reason for questioning line should emerge clearly. 4) Cross-examination. Apart from Brutus, Cassius, Antony, should attack *one* major weakness. There is no need to cross-examine every witness.

Clearly, the preparation is the most important part of the work. While it is going on, the teacher is consultant expert available to all. One advantage of the work is the scope it gives for individual help. Pupils are shown how to work out meaning from the notes of whatever edition they have, but they are encouraged to consult the expert on any difficulties. In practice, since teams are anxious not to leave themselves open to having misreadings exposed by their opponents, there is continual training in interpretation going on. It is wise also to check over question-lines with counsel. A not surprising tendency is for questioning to be unnecessarily long, and most counsel need help with sharpening and tightening an examination. Opening and closing speeches, however, are left to counsel to work out for themselves; the only advice given is that the central basis of argument should come out very clearly.

The trial

Preparation usually takes three to four weeks. The trial proper takes the conventional shape—case for the prosecution, case for the defence, summing-up, jury decision. The judge has absolute authority; he rules on objections, keeps order, intervenes if a witness is being bullied, asks counsel, if necessary, to explain the purpose of his questions. The role of the jury is peculiar to this court; they are already familiar with the facts of the case and have discussed their meaning; they may question witnesses on the meaning of their words, and may raise questions not raised by counsel. The judge, however, may refuse to allow their questions. They reach a decision by majority verdict, to avoid the trial lasting forever. They have three decisions to choose from—guilty, not guilty, not proven.

The liveliness of the trial depends on the energy of counsel and the acting of the witnesses. It is now that good casting pays off. The witnesses try to bring out clearly the roles they are playing, as much as possible using actual words of the characters. Laughter in court is a necessary safety-valve; tempers can run high. The witness playing the Citizen—one is enough—should be one source.

The trial method concentrates attention on one character as he appears to himself and to those around him. It is concerned with searching out the 'why' of choice of action made within the play. That is why Brutus, not Cassius, is put on trial; Cassius has already chosen before the play begins. Again, the choice of action needs to be morally ambiguous; clearly the method does not suit every play. It works well with *Richard II* and *1 Henry IV*. Either Richard or Bolingbroke can be indicted for treason—one for the abuse of kingly power, the other for usurping the crown. It is a way of introducing pupils to the concept of kingship in Shakespeare. Prince Hal can be charged with unfitness to be heir-apparent. With a senior class an interesting version can be tried with *Coriolanus*: the factions of power—tribunes as well as patricians and generals—put on trial for exposing the state to danger. The trial method is not an appropriate way of approaching character in the major tragedies. With these, the method can result in losing sight of elements vital to an understanding of the tragic hero, such as dramatic mode, structure, language-scape.

Characterization in the comedies

Trial by jury would not at all be a way of studying characters in the 'happy' comedies. A preliminary demonstration like that described for *Julius Caesar* I. iii might be used to initiate pupils into how to keep a note-book record. But for a full study of characterization a different approach is needed. With these plays it is a matter of observing behaviour rather than of exploring motive, of recognizing the response of feeling rather than the dispute of reason. What one wants to increase is the pleasure of watching a variety of characters in a variety of situations which surprise them into self-revelation and perhaps self-discovery. Pleasure is important. 'One effect of Shakespeare's comedies is to make us think better of mankind'**(25),** and it would be a pity if the study was not a cheerful enterprise.

One of the features of these plays is Shakespeare's 'ability to involve himself with a great variety of characters without identifying himself with one of them'**(26)**. Thus the study, I think, should keep attention on the variety rather than confine it to hero or heroine. To reinforce the sense of a community of characters, the second reading, like the first, would be a group reading. This time certain moments of the play are set in slow motion, and pupils are shown how to examine these moments closely and to notice the various ways Shakespeare has of revealing character—parallel of gesture and situation, scene sequence, stage-picture. For beginners pacing is important in this connection. The various strategies are gradually introduced. In planning the study, one decides what parts of the play will best show beginners how a certain dramatic strategy throws light on the characters under scrutiny.

Note-book records are written up after each act or sequence of scenes. Guide questions and thinking points indicate the shape of an entry and help pupils to sort out their ideas.

The particular play will suggest a unifying theme for holding the study together—masks in *Twelfth Night*, various kinds of wooing in *As You Like It*, forms of deception in *Much Ado About Nothing*.

Studying characterization in *Twelfth Night*

In the discussion that follows the first reading, there is always disagreement about the treatment of Malvolio, some members feeling that he gets what he deserves, some objecting to the cruelty of the joke played on him. It is a good moment for starting up discussion of the different interpretations possible for other characters also**(27)**. Does Orsino deserve Viola? What sort of marriage will Sir Toby and Maria have? This is the moment too for raising the question of the subtitle, "what you will". The aim is to stimulate interest in the "many sorts of [human] music" in the play and to give readers confidence in the value of their own response. The question of the first reading was—'what dost thou know' about events? The question of the second is—'what dost thou know' about conduct, attitudes, values?

Before starting on a second reading, I should test reaction to Feste, a character who seldom becomes clear to young readers in the first reading. A way of giving him substance is to tell the class about Robert Armin and how his joining the Globe company influenced Shakespeare's way of using the Fool(**28**). The notion of an actual popular star actor gives them a grip on the enigmatic Feste.

The web of reflections and connections in *Twelfth Night* is particularly fine. How much can be taken into account varies according to the reach of the class. In the outline that follows, asterisked questions are intended for brighter pupils.

Act I "What country, friends, is this?"

Before reading, tell the class to watch how Shakespeare assembles his characters, the different way he has of introducing each. Remind them to listen for hints of how the characters react to one another.

For slow motion: the encounter between Viola and Olivia. Canvass suggestions for producing the unveiling, and the willow-cabin speech.

I should include II. i in this act. The effect on the audience of seeing Sebastian immediately after Olivia's falling in love with Viola might be discussed orally. I should raise the question of the age of the four lovers here. Pupils seldom realize without prompting that three of the lovers are not very much older than themselves.

Note-book work:

1) First impressions

Think about the way we first meet Orsino and Viola—their situation, what they are thinking and feeling, how they react to their companions. What difference do you notice between them?

We hear a great deal about Olivia before we meet her. How does what we have heard match what we see for ourselves?

*Why does Shakespeare hold back Olivia's first appearance for so long?

Collect information given about what characters look like.

*What signal is there in so much detail about outside appearance?

2) Relationships

"My desires, like fell and cruel hounds,/Pursue me", says Orsino. How many other characters are in the same situation? Which desires are reasonable? Which are fantastic?

*"You are sick of self-love, Malvolio." Is he the only character in love with himself?

Viola is already in love with Orsino when she comes to Olivia. How does this knowledge affect the way we respond to scene v?

Try to listen to Viola in scene v as if you were Olivia. Why should Olivia fall in love with Viola? Whose side are you on here? What two characters clearly dislike one another intensely in Act I?

*"Misprision in the highest degree!" says Feste. Read this as a signal to Feste's special role in the play. How is the signal strengthened in what follows immediately?

Act II "Disguise, I see, thou art a wickedness."

Before reading, set discussion going on how given we all are to creating masks for ourselves. Tell the class to watch how Shakespeare plays with different versions of this common human practice, from Viola's disguise of her sex to Malvolio's day-dream of an exalted position.

The function of music in the play might be discussed here too. With many groups Feste's songs work better as poems, but it is worth trying the effect of a good recording. The Deller versions are exquisite(**29**). A nice problem for a good class is the notion that the songs are masks created by Feste.

Whether the notion of language-masks is raised depends on the class. If pupils still need a great deal of chorus-work to get past the language-barrier, then it is a matter best left alone. Pupils who are at ease with Shakespeare's language can be set thinking about obvious differences in the way characters talk—Orsino's elaborateness, for instance, or Sir Andrew's fatuousness. Only particularly perceptive pupils are likely to enjoy more subtle variations. A good guide is response during the first reading to the meeting between Viola and Feste (III.i). Most beginners, not surprisingly, find the scene unnecessary and the language largely incomprehensible. More experienced readers enjoy the "by the church" joke and Feste's begging, and are ready to argue the question of how Feste sees Viola; but many are not greatly interested in the exchanges about language or in Viola's reflection on Fools. Those readers who do enjoy these elements are certainly able to take up the question of "corrupters of words" throughout the play.

For slow motion: Viola telling Orsino the 'history' of a girl's love.

Note-book work:

1) The masks

What kind of mask does Sir Andrew try to stick together? Show that he keeps adding new details to it.

Malvolio has two masks—a public and a private. List the features of each.

How does Orsino see himself? What means does he use to persuade the world of the same view?

Are the three aware of their masks? *How are the three linked by the masks they wear?

2) The masks and relationships

What has Sir Toby to do with Sir Andrew's mask?

What effect has Malvolio's public mask on Sir Toby and Maria? What is the consequence for Malvolio of his private mask?

Is Viola happy with her disguise? What consequences has it in her relationship with the Illyrians?

How does Orsino's mask affect his attitude to other people?

3) Behind the masks

The audience can always see behind the masks. Can the characters on the stage do this? What have the masks to do with the 'desires' in Act I?

How does Viola's share in the dialogue (sc. iv) make Orsino's mask obvious? Does Orsino forget his mask at any point?

Feste enjoys stripping off masks. How many instances can you find in Acts I and II?

*The songs link two very different sets of masks. Is it altogether a matter of contrast?

Act III "Misprision in the highest degree"

One would want, I think, to bring any group to delight in the virtuosity of this central movement of the play, where the stage-craft so brilliantly lights up the assembly of characters. Before reading, the class might be set watching for two things in particular: how much closer we come to the truth of individual characters; how the grouping sends out constant waves of information. The amount of noticing expected needs to be matched to the particular group.

For slow motion: Viola and Olivia (sc. i), Viola and Antonio (sc. iv).

Note-book work:

1) Masks and manners

List the misunderstandings and the kind of mask that causes each.

How is Sir Andrew's mask getting on? Any new pieces? Where does he get them?

Notice Sir Toby's manner with Viola. What character does his elaborate speech link him with?

There is a difference in the way Olivia and Sir Toby treat Malvolio. How does this affect our understanding of the two characters?

Up to this Malvolio has worn his two masks separately. What happens now? With what result?

2) Masks and feelings

There is a great variety of feeling in this act. How many different emotions can you identify? Match characters to each emotion. What surprises are there in the way characters are grouped as a result?

How often is it a mask which causes the revelation of feeling?

The biggest cluster of emotions comes at the end of the act. How many can you identify from Antonio's entry in scene iv to the end of the scene?

*Frequently, there are different degrees of the same emotion. For example, a line of contempt rises and falls throughout the act. In scene i, the line rises from Feste's cool contempt towards Viola, through Sir Toby's hostile contempt towards her at the gates, to Viola's "contempt and anger" towards Olivia. In scene ii the line drops to Sir Toby's and Fabian's contempt towards Sir Andrew. In scene iii, the line rises from Maria's mocking contempt towards Malvolio to Malvolio's fierce contempt for Sir Toby and company. In scene iv, the line reaches its highest point in Antonio's bitter contempt for the ingratitude of which he thinks Sebastian is guilty. Try tracing the variation of degree in some of the following emotions—desire, anxiety, anger, disappointment, surprise.

3) Stage-craft

Examine the stage-picture when Antonio names Sebastian. If you were producing the play, what directions would you give to each actor at this point?

*"... out of my welkin, I might say 'element'", says Feste. "I am not of your element", says Malvolio. What information does the echo convey?

*"I hate ingratitude more in a man/Than lying, vainness, babbling, drunkenness,/Or any taint of vice whose strong corruption/Inhabits our frail blood." What kind of signal to the audience is this?

Acts IV and V "Take and give back affairs and their dispatch
With such a smooth, discreet, and stable bearing"

The last two acts can be taken together. Tell the class to watch how characters meet the consequences of their choice of conduct, how masks disintegrate, how the balance is held between danger and happiness.

Note-book work:

1) "Are all the people mad?"

Notice the number of times madness is spoken of. There are several kinds of madness represented. Identify the madness of Feste, Sebastian, Malvolio, Olivia, Orsino, Antonio, Viola. Does a pattern emerge?

2) What you will

Viola, Orsino, Olivia, Sebastian, Malvolio are all faced with a serious decision connected with their desires. How does the way a character responds to the challenge suggest the truth of what the character is?

What characters show real anger in Acts IV and V? Have there been other links between any of these characters before this?

Level of ironic counterpoint: *1 Henry IV*

A problem with the history plays is that they reflect a political structure alien to the experience of young readers. Certain ideas peculiar to that structure do not make much sense to the middle-year pupils likely to meet these plays: the sacredness of the King, the location of authority in one man, the hierarchy of degree, the wrongness of rebellion. The danger is that rejection of these ideas may obscure the other side of the case, the fact that 'the issues Shakespeare raised are still with us, still awaiting the answers he never finally gave'**(30)**. If the history plays are to be studied in the classroom, it is Shakespeare's power to make the audience judge what is going on that should, I think, guide the teaching approach. It is not a matter of profundity of judgement but of recognition that there are relevant moral and political questions asked by the plays. Reading a history play is an introduction to the notion of the theatre as a place where the private man is set thinking about public affairs.

1 Henry IV provides an excellent opportunity for opening the level of ironic counterpoint, of how much the pattern of characterization has to do with our interest in what is going on**(31)**. The first reading aims at a clear grasp of what happens and the way the narrative is shaped. The second reading focuses attention on the characters—those who make the events happen and those who are caught up in the consequences.

A starting-point for the second reading might be discussion of the fact that this play about great public events is very much concerned with individual behaviour. Set the class as a group exercise to recall how fond the characters are of criticizing one another's behaviour. There is hardly one who does not indulge in the practice. The King's analysis of his own and his son's behaviour is at the centre of a pattern of comment expressed in admiration or contempt, anger or mockery, imitation or parody. Recording group findings would be a first stage in building up individual annotation.

The important thing to keep in mind is the questioning of Shakespeare's 'two eyed scrutiny'**(30)**; to help pupils enjoy the ironic counterpointing that is a dominant feature of how the play was made. The first reading makes clear one kind of grouping—the court, the rebels, the tavern. The second reading aims at recognition of a kinship of behaviour which suggests new groupings. Certain categories would indicate how to record these. For instance, motive for action might be one category. This way of grouping would reveal Falstaff and Hotspur in one group and the Bolingbrokes and Worcester in another. Again, the category of personal ambition would reveal a kinship between the King and Hotspur, while that of ambition for the good of the state would show a kinship between the King and the Prince.

A central question is the role of honour in how history is made. I should start the question where Shakespeare starts it—in particular behaviour and attitudes, not general concepts. The individuality of the characters and their responsibility for the health of the state are largely defined in the way they use the ability to lie: from Falstaff's rich exploitation of this power of language to delight himself, his companions and the audience, to Worcester's vicious and destructive abuse of the power; from the King's concealment of his real ambition to Hotspur's confusion of heroics with rebellion against the order of the state, from Falstaff's shamming dead to Sir Walter Blunt's self-sacrificing disguise; from the Prince's playing the part of his father to his trying on the role of Hotspur. To work out the hierarchy of pretence in the play is an exercise which causes pupils to think about the Prince. At first hearing, the soliloquy "I know you all . . ." usually provokes blank condemnation. A way of countering prejudice is to suggest that we are watching Hal in the process of learning what it means to be a future king, of finding for himself a right way of behaving. Where in this England is he to find a model? In the King? In Falstaff? In Hotspur? What does he learn from his observation of the three?

The last act is the moment for reviewing "what is in that word honour". Is Sir Walter's merely "a grinning honour" as Falstaff would have it? Is Falstaff's "Give me life" sufficient answer to the busy quest for honour? Has the Prince "cropped" honour in his defeat of Hotspur? Does Shakespeare mean that Hotspur's kind of honour is quite worthless when his dead body is occasion for another bit of Falstaff's shamelessness? What judgement of "civil strife" is implied in Falstaff's portrait of the soldiers he leads to battle? What honour is the King left with? In the end, "Who hath it?"

Character in *Romeo and Juliet*

Because the play is 'a tragedy of youth as youth sees it'**(17)**, the young can bring to *Romeo and Juliet* an intuitive knowledge keener than they can bring, at this stage, to any other Shakespeare play. Identification with the two lovers can have a personal immediacy; the experience may indeed be 'adding meaning and sanctification to their little loves'**(32)**. It is an occasion for special teaching tact, for taking care not to stand in the light, for being aware that the pupils may be the true experts of the simplicity of the love which is so much a wonder of the play—that freedom from adult questioning, doubts, hesitations. We do well not to lose sight of the fact that it is the only play in the canon which truly has a child as heroine. Shakespeare chose to make Juliet fourteen, not sixteen as she is in his source. It is a child that Romeo falls in love with. At the end, we are reminded of the central importance of that youthfulness when Shakespeare puts a frightened child on the stage—Paris's page.

To study character in this play is to enter the 'shared private world of intensity created by the two lovers'**(33)**, and to see it against the blindness of the surrounding world, the world of those whose view of love is not enlightened by experience of it. Whatever the production-slant of the first reading, it can hardly fail to bring out the isolation of the lovers, the inviolability of the world they create—a world still intact at the end of the play. The second reading aims at surer recognition of the two worlds: on the one hand, the lineaments of the lovers' experience; on the other hand, the activity of the everyday world which affects their destiny though it cannot affect their love. Both worlds are well within the imaginative reach of adolescents; the first because of their intuitive equipment, the second because of the "sound substantial flesh and blood" of the two characters who stand out in the everyday world—Mercutio and the Nurse. A good professional recording works very well for this second reading(**34**). The pupils listen to each sequence, following the text in their books, and then do the note-book work described.

There are two sections for each stage of the note-book record:

A The two lovers. The emphasis is on the transforming power of love. From the moment they love, the lovers enter an intensified life of feeling where the casual, the neutral response to being alive is no longer possible. Romeo's "O she doth teach the torches to burn bright", points to a transformation as radical as it is immediate. The changed situation brings with it the responsibility of choice. The love itself is not the result of decision; it is enough that they should see each other. But external circumstances constantly force them into decisions in an effort to hold safe the private world created by love. They are compelled to oppose the irresponsible activity around them by responsible action. An important part of the study is how the lovers grow as they meet every new threat.

B The surrounding world: The outer world is peopled by characters always in motion. Here observation is concentrated on Mercutio and the Nurse, both of whom burst the constraint of stylization that marks treatment of other characters. In both there is scope for recognizing how each is at once unique and representative.

Outline of Study

Note: It would be wise first to discuss orally sections marked *.

Act I Scenes i–iv: *The Two Households*

A 1) Romeo's life before he meets Juliet. How he sees himself. How other characters see him. How the audience sees him. *Point of his not being involved in the quarrel.

2) Juliet's life before she meets Romeo. Her father's description, "My child is yet a stranger in the world". Her relationship with the Nurse. Her response to the suggestion of marriage.

B Mercutio and the Nurse: The kind of person each is. Mercutio in *action.* The way the Nurse speaks as well as what she says. Attitude of each to love.

Act I Scene v and Act II: *"So smile the heavens"*

A 1) The first meeting: The sudden transformation of two lives. What happens to each in the moment of seeing the other. *The mutuality of the experience expressed through the sonnet-dialogue. The release of happiness. Juliet at discovery of her lover's identity.

2) The Balcony scene: This scene might be approached differently. Set the pupils to listen to it again, and then, without further reference to the text, to describe the scene as it now lives in their imagination. Accuracy of memory may be checked later, misquotations corrected, and further discoveries added.

3) "The measure of joy". Waiting for the union of marriage. Romeo with his friends now. Juliet waiting for the Nurse's return, Juliet with the Nurse. The coming together.

B Mercutio and the Nurse. Relationship with the lovers—Mercutio's with Romeo, the Nurse's with Juliet. Individuality of each character—self-sufficiency, energy, enjoyment of life etc. *The two as together representing the gulf between the private world of the lovers and the common world.

Act III Scenes i–iv: "*This day's black fate*"

A How the lovers meet the reversal of fortune.

1) Romeo. Attitude to the Mercutio/Tybalt quarrel. Decisiveness at news of Mercutio's death. Behaviour at the news of banishment.

2) Juliet. Waiting for the Nurse—"Gallop apace" etc. Anguish and confusion at the Nurse's news. Choice.

3) *Each has been charged with speaking out of true in this sequence—Juliet's condemnation of Romeo; Romeo's hysteria in the friar's cell.

B Mercutio. His provocation of the quarrel—surprising or predictable? Degree of his responsibility for his death. How he meets death.

The Nurse. How she breaks the news to Juliet—surprising or predictable? How much does she understand?

Act III Scene v – Act IV: "*That siege of grief*"

A 1) The Parting Scene. A similar approach to that used for the Balcony scene. Tell the class to listen to how the scene both recalls the Balcony scene and contrasts with it: the mutuality of feeling now deepened by passion; images—bird, light, stars—now with changed significance; how the lovers see each other's faces now.

2) Juliet alone. How she meets each new betrayal—her father's anger, her mother's refusal of sympathy, the Nurse's failure to understand her need. The clearness with which she sees her own isolation. Her sureness of purpose in the Friar's cell. *The potion speech: the quick imagination here—child's and adult's. What at last restores her courage.

B The Nurse: Her failure of Juliet—in character? Last view of the Nurse—discovery of Juliet dead. How much of her is there in this moment?

Act V: "*This bed of death*"

A 1) Romeo alone. His state before he hears of Juliet's death. His response to the news as against his response to the news of banishment.

2) The Apothecary episode. Signs of a new maturity in Romeo. *Recall Juliet alone: how does the figure of the Apothecary link the two lovers?

3) *The last scene. How the scene is an image of the whole tragic story. Romeo's last actions as collaboration with fate. Echoes in his last speech of earlier moments, both joyful and tragic. Juliet's awakening—"O *comfortable* Friar", "Where is Romeo?", "O happy dagger".

B *"There where the torch doth burn". The repeopling of the stage after Juliet's death. The long ending.

Using note-book material

Note-book work needs to be followed up by a practical demonstration of its value. In the case of *Julius Caesar*, the trial proper is such a demonstration. Oral practice in using the material assembled is also necessary for other kinds of note-book work. One form is the panel discussion. This method has the advantage that pupils share their insights, so that a number of aspects of the play can be covered relatively quickly. The discussions are an excellent preparation for dealing with the type of question that appears on examination papers.

The class is divided into panels of five or six experts. Each panel is assigned a topic and set to collect relevant material, using the note-books as a source. Individual members are responsible for different aspects of a given topic. Topics are so designed as to demand taking the play as a whole into account. This is the moment for setting the pupils thinking about values. The characters are 'not presented in a moral vacuum; the themes which are embodied in the plays all constitute a criticism of life, and it is hardly rash to assume that the poet intended this criticism to be understood by his audience'**(35)**.

Each panel gives a short account of its findings. Then the discussion is opened to the rest of the class, who may question the experts, challenge their findings, offer insights of their own. Unless the class is particularly advanced, the teacher chairs each discussion.

Sample questions for panel discussion

Twelfth Night

1) The happiness of *Twelfth Night*

What happiness means for the different characters. True and false notions of happiness. Reasons for success or failure in the quest for happiness. Any characters incapable of being happy?

2) 'Comic plots are made up of changes, chances and surprise'**(36)**.

Is there a scene without these elements? How much are the characters themselves responsible for what happens? Is Illyria a never-never land or our world disguised?

3) "Dost thou think because thou art virtuous, there shall be no more cakes and ale?"

The view of life represented by Sir Toby, by Malvolio. Is either view given total approval in the play? Any sense in which Sir Toby and Malvolio are alike? The view of life represented by Feste.

4) Strangers in Illyria

Viola, Sebastian, Antonio. What have the three in common? Do they fit easily into Illyria? Does their arrival import any new values?

5) A family of characters

Links and echoes between characters—situation, masks, manners, desires, mistakes, reactions. Any character who coincides at no point with any other character?

6) "A fair behaviour"

Courtesy, truth, compassion, generosity, courage in the play. How different characters measure up to these ideals.

1 Henry IV

1) "How this world is given to lying"

Purpose and consequences of the various forms of counterfeit and role-playing. Number of plays within the play.

2) "Banish plump Jack and banish all the world"

The charm of Falstaff. Could he be spared from the play? His presence as a criticism of other characters and of events.

3) The Prince and Falstaff

Relationship between the two. The Prince's judgement of Falstaff. How well does Falstaff know the Prince?

4) "What is honour?"

Versions of honour from the King, the Prince, Hotspur, Falstaff. Connection between honour and courage. Is Falstaff without courage?

5) "All-abhorred war"

Attitude to war of those in high places. "Danger and disobedience". Causes of rebellion in present and past. Consequences of rebellion.

6) "Days of villainy"

Political disturbance, social conditions, lawlessness in lord and commoner. Where does responsibility for the state of England lie?

Romeo and Juliet

1) "Poor sacrifices of our enmity"

Prologue as exploration of the tragedy. Ancient grudge and present anger. Amount of thoughtless violence. Connections between other people's quarrelling and the lovers' story. Triumph of love.

2) "Fortune's fool"

Chance and accident throughout. Are characters wholly at the mercy of fate? Responsibility of characters for events.

3) Love's transformation

Speed of love. Discovering a new world, and new powers in themselves. Changed view of the old world. Growth of the two lovers.

4) The two worlds

Outside world's misunderstanding of love. How scene sequence and stage-picture constantly reveal contrast between the two worlds. Point at which contrast becomes collision.

5) "Rich in beauty"

Unforgettable parts of the play. The language of love.

6) "Day in night"

Images of light and dark throughout. How these are used to convey harmony or discord, joy or agony.

5

Understanding Shakespeare

'Tragedy implies a whole view of the universe'(**37**). 'Nothing less than the limits of man's nature is under scrutiny'(**38**). 'Reading Shakespeare is a perpetual discovery of ourselves'(**39**). 'Shakespeare just enlivens life, no matter how futile you think it is, in a way nobody else has been able to do'(**40**).

Two facts stand out in all the thinking about Shakespeare that has been recorded over the centuries. On the one hand, the size of his achievement, the comprehensiveness of his vision and the craftsmanship which could give that vision sensible life. On the other, his accessibility to all sorts of receivers, the continuing power of the plays to tempt us out of the narrow circle of our own preoccupations. Both facts are relevant to what happens when we are responsible for guiding new readers through one of the major tragedies. We are dealing with work of daunting complexity, with 'an immensely inclusive anthropology'(**41**). We are also dealing with experience which matters profoundly in the growth of those we are teaching. It is of utmost importance that we should not underestimate the capacity of the young to find themselves in their encounters with the work. Certainly, we have the responsibility of training students to be reasonably articulate about a text set for examination. But that is not the whole of the matter. There is also the more humanly important factor of a growth in consciousness and responsiveness to human experience. That such growth is not measurable does not make it less important. When what lies between us and a class is a great work of art, there needs to be space for what cannot be explicitly stated; an awareness of what cannot be measured, of the fact that in this situation students can see and hear far more than they can express in words.

I have begun to use the word 'student' instead of 'pupil'. Up to now, what we have been concerned with was the gradual introduction of a new audience to various levels of a Shakespeare play. In this chapter, we are concerned with that audience at the moment when the members can become students of Shakespeare. They now bring to a play the equipment acquired through their previous experience as well as their own naturally increasing maturity. Independence of response is important at any stage, but the degree of independence that can now be expected is very much finer. 'Any play exists for you to the extent that *you* have grappled with its meanings'(**42**). The aim with a senior class is to lead the students to independent grappling with a masterpiece. The final stage of the work is the *Notes for a new production*, which is the individual record of a student's thinking about the play.

The level of language

The meanings to be grappled with are the meanings of a play, and how students are helped to grapple with them is still firmly based on that fact. But there is a dimension which takes on a greater importance at this stage. I think most of us would agree that to read one of the great tragedies with a senior class is to be aware of a change in the kind of response that occurs. One senses a new openness to the play's 'extra-theatrical truth'(**43**). The response is natural; it is the consequence of an increased capacity for being moved by the 'imaginative *charge* of the language'(**44**). Shakespeare is a great poet as well as a great playwright. His genius 'is a genius for language above all; it was that which enabled him to embody any conception he entertained'(**45**). He lives on the page as well as in the theatre, and it is not, I suggest, our business to campaign for one existence over the other. Both are important in grappling with the meanings. The level of enjoyment we now want to open explicitly is that of language.

This closer attention to the language does not mean examining the play in the manner of the textual scholar. As always, what matters in the classroom is the *first-hand* experience available to the students. It is the living power of the poetry to bring about understanding that is in question. F. P. Wilson's reminder to scholars is relevant, 'While we strive to make ourselves Shakespeare's contemporaries, it is even more important to make Shakespeare our contemporary, to keep him level with life and with our lives'(**25**). There is just one sense in which we can encourage students to be Shakespeare's contemporaries: by developing something of the Elizabethan capacity for listening. There is time in the classroom and in private reading for this as there is not in the theatre. To learn to listen is to come to discover that the true illuminating close-up in a Shakespeare play is the language. One of the drawbacks in TV as a medium for Shakespeare is that the inevitable close-ups of a character's face draw attention away from the language he is speaking.

Again, it is not necessary to make a technical study of versification. There is not time to equip students with enough knowledge of prosody to make it a useful tool in grappling with the meanings. An awareness of the relationship between rhythmic movement and meaning can be developed in passages where the relationship is obvious. For example, the difference of movement between Hamlet's "O what a rogue and peasant slave am I" soliloquy and his "To be or not to be" soliloquy; the increasing feverishness of stress in Leontes's expression of the surge of his jealousy. There are occasions where the ability to identify metre can illuminate meaning, and the matter may be introduced at the teacher's discretion. In *King Lear* I should want students to hear the difference between the splendid rhetoric the royal Lear commands and the plainness of his most memorable utterances, where the metrical line is freed to the point that we do not hear it at all. The difference enables understanding of Lear's own quest for meaning. For students, the scene which best makes this clear is the Awakening scene; there the language escapes from the conventional distinctions between verse and prose to a purity of utterance which seems to be neither. We listen intently to every word as Lear gropes for the "modest truth". It is only when we analyze it afterwards that we realize that he has, in fact, used verse which is metrically as modest as the truth he discovers.

The chief aim is to develop the ability to recognize the particular language-scape of a play as an essential guide to meanings**(46)**. Noticing images and iterations is part of the work at an earlier stage. At the senior stage it can be taken explicitly a good deal further. In the great tragedies this feature of Shakespeare's way of building the world of the play is available for students at first-hand. It is usually enough simply to start them listening for them to notice the language-mode of the hero and the world he inhabits. Another feature to make explicit is how dramatic images come to life in a way peculiar to drama: they frequently pass out of language into spectacle. In *Macbeth*, murdered sleep becomes visible in the Sleepwalking scene. In *King Lear*, spiritual blindness has its physical counterpart. In *Othello*, Iago's "I follow him" is visible as well as figurative.

Background knowledge at senior stage

The test of what background information to give students is whether the information truly helps them in their grappling with the play. The objection to much secondary material is that it must be second-hand. Information about Elizabeth revenge plays can hardly be accompanied by experience of an example. Does such information really affect how we experience *Hamlet*? 'Tragedy shakes us with its tremendous *here* and *now* (no matter how remote its subjects)'**(47)**. What we need to ask is whether particular background material will get in the way of the *here* and *now*, make the play, in fact, remote. Sometimes background information is valuable. I have found it profitable to read *Everyman* first with a class which is going to study *King Lear*. The first-hand experience of a morality play makes clearer certain otherwise puzzling features of Shakespeare's play.

There is one aspect of historical background which cannot be ignored at this stage—the moral and cultural context within which Shakespeare lived and worked**(48)**. Students need to have a grasp of historical perspective if they are not to get bogged down in irrelevant considerations. The knowledge required varies from play to play, and from group to group. An awareness of the accepted attitude to sexual morality—promiscuity, chastity before marriage, marital fidelity—is important for *Othello*, *Hamlet*, *The Winter's Tale*. The Christian belief in the dual nature of man—creature of earth and eternity—is essential knowledge for the major tragedies, in particular for *King Lear* and *Macbeth*. So is knowledge of the accepted structure of relationships—parent and child, husband and wife, king and subject, master and servant. Generally, it is not difficult to convey sufficient knowledge of such ideas for the purposes of a given play. A sense of historical perspective is a natural development at this stage, and is being aided by experience of other literature—the 19th century novel, for instance. There are, of course, occasions when one may decide not to raise certain questions at all, simply because there is not enough time for dealing with them properly. *Othello* provides an example. Desdemona's obedience to Othello cannot be passed over; students will raise the question themselves, anyway. But the question of Iago's resemblance to the Devil is more complex. It is not merely a matter of whether he has cloven feet, and for many students nowadays that may be what A. N. Whitehead calls 'an inert idea'**(49)**, and so better left alone.

Shakespeare's stage

Another kind of background material is information about the kind of theatre Shakespeare was writing for. Quite young classes are fascinated by the working conditions of the Globe, but it cannot be claimed that the knowledge is active when they are reading a play. For senior pupils certain features can be illuminating, for example, the continuity of performance, the absence of breaks between scenes and acts. Actually, this is one feature which it is natural to reproduce in the classroom at any stage; the breaking-up into acts and scenes need be seen as no more than convenient for textual reference.

There is one undisputed feature of the Globe stage which is worth making part of visualization—its shape**(50)**. How Shakespeare made his apron stage serve meaning is frequently important to understanding. The width and depth allowed great variety of grouping and movement; it allowed a character to come close to the audience in a special way, to step, in a sense, out of the play. Awareness of this gives a new plausibility to the aside and to the device of concealment. There is a relationship between the stage space and the visualization demanded by the language. Lady Macbeth can fill the air with dark spirits because at that moment she has the whole space of the stage at her command. The battlements of Elsinore are the more imaginable because of the emptiness in which they are evoked. Bernardo has too much room for comfort.

Visualization of the stage Shakespeare had in his mind's eye when writing is extremely helpful in reading *Othello* and *King Lear*. Throughout *Othello* the stage-picture comments on Othello and Iago and on the relationship between them. Consider what we see physically. Six times during the first two acts the stage holds only two characters—Iago and a victim, but not Iago and Othello; there are servants present for the Othello/Iago dialogue in I.ii. Iago's power to come close to Othello is thus held in suspense. Throughout these two acts Othello is always seen at the centre of a well-filled stage. The group frequently includes Iago, or rather has Iago at the edge. He joins Othello at the centre only at Othello's invitation, always in a way which shocks the audience but not the group: when Othello sends him for Desdemona, confides Desdemona to his care, demands an explanation of the brawl. Othello's stature, freedom, openness are thus theatrically emphasized, so that when in III.iii the stage holds only Othello and Iago, the new visual experience surprises us into heightened attention. In the middle of the scene, for the first time in the play, the stage holds only Othello. This new picture, coming where it does, implies that Othello is facing the first profound testing of his integrity, and at the same time gives the measure of Iago's power. The two are seen alone together for the last time in IV.i. In this scene the stage-picture emphasizes Othello's enslavement in the way the Iago/Roderigo dialogues are recalled at the beginning and end of the scene, in Othello's collapse at Iago's feet, in Othello's taking a stage-position up to now peculiarly Iago's—the spy at the edge of the group. An Iago-like secretiveness is again suggested in Othello's brief appearance in V.i; this appearance exploits our memory of Othello's very different behaviour on similar occasions earlier in the play, in I.ii and II. iii. After IV.i, Othello and Iago are drawn apart again. Iago returns to his original stage-mode of the first two acts. Othello advances alone to the first private scene with Desdemona and to the terrible privacy of the murder. The stage-picture thus throws weight on his responsibility for his crime, on his new isolation, and makes it possible to restore his stature. Finally, he is at the centre of a group again, which shows as well as says the beginning of the end. Iago is present, but now he is unable to choose those exits and entrances which have been so much a part of his stage-movement.

In the opening scene of *King Lear*, the size of the stage makes possible a double picture which immediately establishes the relationship between the main plot and the subplot. The double picture—the little group in ordinary conversation and the elaborate court group which follows—pays enormous dividends in audience involvement. The first casual picture takes the audience easily towards the stage, so that when Kent breaks into the second picture to stand "between the Dragon and his wrath", he draws the audience with him into the huge world of the play. There is another way in which Shakespeare exploits the size of the stage in *King Lear* which seems to me highly significant. When the court image of the opening scene is shattered, what takes its place is the open world.

Lear literally does not find shelter again "from the disasters of the world". Most editions provide a Hall in Albany's palace for I.iv. But the text gives no warrant for this setting. All we know is that Lear is returning from hunting. The only sure exception is the scene in Gloucester's farmhouse, a bitterly ironic version of the Court scene. What is significant there is that Lear is carried *out* from the house: he cannot have the shelter of even so rough and poor a place. The predominant open-air setting is reinforced in the evocation of place after the break-up of the court-image: the heath, Tom o' Bedlam's countryside and hovel, the sea, the acres at Dover, the unseen prison. A final point: when Cordelia at the end of the Awakening scene says "Will't pleasure your Highness walk?", she is inviting him *in* to shelter, redeeming the "opposed bolts" of the Storm scene.

Secondary reading

Another question to consider is the introduction of secondary material of a critical kind. The test again is whether such reading enlivens the students' understanding. If following critical thinking does not fire their own thinking, then it is a futile exercise. Generally, students are stimulated by the encounter with critical reflection on a work they know and love. How much and what reading to recommend depends on the particular teaching situation. There are some good specially designed commentaries which meet the needs of most students(**51**). Exceptional students can be encouraged to explore the leading critics at first hand(**52**). Reading critical work should follow, not precede, reading the play. In the same context, I do not think the play should be prefaced with a discourse on theories of tragedy. First, one can deal with the subject only at a level so reductive as to falsify it. Second, the students have experience at best of only two or three plays, which is not sufficient material for comparative reflection. Third, and most important, each tragedy has its own 'logic of tragic suffering'(**38**) to be discovered in first-hand experience and study of the particular play.

Reading the play

Since there is less need for choric intervention, the play-reading stage with senior students does not take long. While it is important to have a production-slant in mind, this can be less emphatically present than with younger classes. Sometimes, indeed, the slant may change in the course of the reading because of the way the play is working on the readers. For example, on one occasion the slant I had in mind for *Hamlet* was Hamlet's intense awareness of all the parts of his world. The impact of the play-within-the-play on the class caused me to change direction. What especially excited interest at that point was the sense of the struggle between Hamlet and Claudius. Response was so strong that the struggle dominated the rest of the reading. Later, when the students were preparing to work on their own *Notes for a new production*, the change in slant was seen as a valid way of producing *Hamlet*: in the first half a hero distinctively open and responsive, in the second a hero whose attention closes round his enemy.

There need not be a second reading like that described in Chapter Four. Instead, there is a series of discussions of various aspects, which involves rereading, both private and group. Discussion aims at opening questions rather than supplying answers. The students' own questions may be the starting-point. These discussions are a working model of the kind of reading that grappling with the play demands. Previous knowledge of how meaning is embodied in a play is reinforced and increased. Inquiry is always inquiry into a work which has visible and audible life. Again, parts will be examined separately, but the examination of a part will always lead to reflection upon its relationship to the whole. I should preface discussion of any play with the reminder that Shakespeare 'is continually spinning threads which he himself delivers into our hands in order that . . . we may understand what follows'. . . . He prepares 'in the mind of the audience a whole net of expectations, intuitions and conjectures . . . Almost every single detail is used later on, reappears suddenly at an important point'**(24)**.

Othello and Iago

The contrasting of major characters is an important element in our understanding of a Shakespeare play. To observe how Claudius is set against Hamlet, Iago against Othello, Edmund against Lear, Macduff or Malcolm against Macbeth, throws light on the whole. This is not a matter of double entry with apt quotations, but of watching the opposition work itself out through all the parts. Since the contrast has meaning only in the context of the whole, it is not examined in isolation from the rest of the play. It is the *growing* stage-history of a contrasted pair which students are invited to observe closely.

In *Othello*, the contrast between Othello and Iago is not simply one way of throwing light on the whole; in a sense, it is the play. To discuss the question is to put the whole play under scrutiny. The contrast is obvious. What discussion focuses on is the dramatic *encounter* of two radically different characters through which the terrifying possibility is explored—that mind can invade mind. "Where's that palace, whereinto foul things/Sometimes intrude not?"

The discussion would have three parts: Acts I and II, Act III, Acts IV and V. The division is a practical necessity and does not preclude ranging backwards and forwards over the play during discussion of a given part. Again, the structure suggested below is not intended to be rigidly followed. In practice, once a class is caught up in discussion, the separate sections frequently overlap, or the order in which points are taken up changes. The students prepare for each part by individual rereading. To make sure that this reading is alive, they are provided with thinking-points beforehand.

Acts I and II

Thinking-points: Preparation of the audience. The two voices. Correspondance and difference between response of the audience and of those on the stage to Othello and Iago. Moments when Othello's sense of the world is clearest; when Iago's view of the world is most disturbing. The stage-picture for these moments. Othello and the gift of joy; Iago and the gift of the moment. Where the following first occur: the notion of honesty, allusion to magic, iteration.

Talking-points:

1) The two voices. Why the slant-technique of the opening scene, the challenge to our wits of the allusive dialogue? Iago must convince as a successful hypocrite. Why then the coarseness of his practising on this first appearance?

Impact of Othello's relative silence in I.ii and his demeanour to Brabantio, in connection with Iago's loquacity and insults in I.i.

Significance of what releases Othello's eloquence in I.iii.

Desdemona in Othello's words. In Iago's words.

Othello's past is a "round unvarnished tale". Iago's past?

Relationship between the two characters. The way in which Othello is present to Iago, Iago to Othello. Can Iago do without Othello?

2) The visage in the mind. The various signals to Othello's "free and open nature". His distinctive idiom; the absence of soliloquy, of a private scene with Desdemona; his reaction to provocation, to violence.

Other voices: Othello in the words of Desdemona, of the Duke and Signiors, of Cassio. Any trace of Brabantio's prejudice?

Visibility of Iago's mind. To other characters—justification of the belief in his honesty. How many voices has Iago in Acts I and II?

How clear a view has the audience? Is it possible to judge the relative weight of envy, hatred, resentment over promotion, racial prejudice, sexual jealousy? His soliloquies—true soliloquies or 'misplaced asides'(**53**)? Repetition of the same knowledge, or gradual clarification of how his "cause is hearted"?

Iago's intelligence. Acuteness of perception—of Othello, of Cassio. What about his reading of Desdemona? Typical observations on human nature. What does he, in fact, know?

3) The two worlds. Othello's response to the gift of the world. A great and experienced soldier. The light thrown by his opening words, by "Keep up your bright swords, for the dew will rust 'em", by "Silence that dreadful bell". The clarity of his moral ideals; the virtues he holds dearest. Precise cause and revelation of the first anger—"My blood begins my safer guides to rule ...". The quality of Othello's love: the meeting in Cyprus. Credibility of Iago's suspicion of "the lustful Moor".

Iago's use of the world. "Poison his delight". The effect on him of goodness and happiness. His view of love. "Put money in thy purse" speech as a paradigm of his response to life. "Pleasure and action, make the hours seem short." Iago's 'pleasure' and 'action'. His strength as a practiser. The first move—"Call up her father"—calculated or improvised? Other instances.

4) Dramatic strategies. Stage-movement and stage-picture—Iago's exits and entrances, his absence during the wooing speech, his presence at the meeting in Cyprus. Oppositions and parallels—other characters besides Othello and Iago. Exploitation of audience knowledge—"You best know the place"; "Honest Iago, my Desdemona must I leave to thee".

Ironies and iterations—"without a prompter", "my life upon her faith", "honest", "free", "poison", "devil", magic, sea.

Act II

Recap of how Shakespeare has prepared for the Temptation scene, how much immediate experience of the two characters the audience brings to the central struggle. This scene of intimate conflict is the point at which the language contrast can most clearly be recognized.

Thinking-points: The first sign of danger. The first use of the word 'jealousy'. Iago's playing of the "perdurable cable", his directing of Othello's thinking. Source of Othello's vulnerability. Othello's collaboration with Iago. When Othello's language begins to show signs of infection. Peak moments.

Talking-points:

1) Apparent continuance along familiar lines of the action. Iago at his daily work. Connection between last lines of Act II and "draw the Moor out of the way". Iago's quickness in seizing the gift of the moment—Cassio's leaving Desdemona, Desdemona's information about Cassio's role in Othello's wooing.

The clarity of the odds: what Othello has to lose; the size of the challenge Iago takes on.

2) Tempter and victim. How much of what we already know of each separately is present in the union of the two? Implications of Othello's *quick* reaction to Iago's "I like not that". Prepared for or a new element? The changing relationship—Iago's "distinct" attack on Desdemona as well as Cassio, his increasing obscenity. Othello's delivery of himself to Iago. For example, the unconscious contradiction in "I'll see before I doubt, when I doubt, prove" is played with by Iago in the variation on 'see' in his answer; the imaginative passion of Othello's farewell to arms inspires the pretended passion of "O Grace, O heaven defend me ...".

The administration of the poison. The timing of each drop from the first 'jealousy' to the incitement to murder. The interspersed drops of commonplace wisdom. The composition of the poison. The working of the poison. The stages of Othello's destruction, from the first unease to the cry for vengeance. The infected language. The two Othellos of the soliloquy. Why place the first Othello soliloquy here?

3) The two worlds. How much of Othello's world does Iago now control? Parts of it beyond his reach?

The language contrast: At a number of points Othello and Iago seem to be saying the same thing—about jealousy, reputation, proof of Desdemona's guilt, cuckoldry. How does the mode of expression maintain the contrast between them—Othello's spontaneity, Iago's calculation; Othello's imagination, Iago's conscious ingenuity?

Implication of Othello's failure to "dissemble" in scene iv. The Othello of the "magic in the web" sequence.

4) The ironies. "My lord shall never rest"; "when I love thee not,/Chaos is come again"; "Show me thy thought"; "You cannot, if my heart were in your hand". The ironies of chance.

Acts IV and V

In IV.i we seem to be at the beginning of the play again, with Othello become a Roderigo. But that cannot be the reality. It is Othello, not Iago's puppet, who must come to his "journey's end".

Thinking-points: The shaping of the final movement. The method of contrast in these acts. Point at which the word 'justice' appears. Othello's madness. Iago's share in what Othello is at his death.

Talking-points:

1) The unlocking of Othello and Iago. Othello as Iago's puppet in IV.i. Contrast between this and the destruction of a "perfect soul" in III.iii. Measure of Iago's power—grotesqueness of the change in Othello. Othello's collapse as a new point of contrast.

"My heart is turn'd to stone . . ."; "the pity of it, Iago, O Iago, the pity of it, Iago!"; "I will chop her into messes . . ."—as the moment of brightest contrast. How the moment contains the whole tragedy.

Iago's last successful prompting—"strangle her in bed"—as also the definitive unlocking. Does the way Othello takes the suggestion coincide with Iago's intention? Iago's 'justice'; Othello's 'justice'. Connection with "It is the cause". Implications of the fact that after this the two are never again seen alone together.

2) Iago's size in these acts. Connection with the first two acts. Significance of the dreadful consistency of his behaviour. Is Iago capable of change? "He has a daily beauty in his life,/That makes me ugly"—new light or old? Point of his refusal to speak after his unmasking?

Desdemona as Iago's opposite.

3) Othello's size in these acts: "This the noble nature,/Whom passion could not shake?"

Connection between the 'blow' sequence and I.iii. Impact of the first scene in which Othello and Desdemona are seen alone together. What Othello sees, what Desdemona sees, what the audience sees. Double irony of "I took you for that cunning whore of Venice".

The last scene. The Othello who enters v.ii. What profound change has taken place since he last crossed the stage? The working of reason, imagination, feeling, senses, in the opening soliloquy. The Othello Desdemona sees in the following dialogue. Signal of "Thou dost *stone* my heart"? The Othello of the murder; immediately after the murder. The Othello Emilia finds; Montano and Gratiano find. The shock of the truth—"Where should Othello go?" "Cold, cold, my girl . . ."; "Steep-down gulfs of liquid fire." The final clarity. Connection with Othello's self-understanding in Act I.

4) "Chaos is come again." The sea-image throughout the play in relation to both characters. The web of contrasts in these acts—light and dark, cold and heat, speed and slowness, stillness and violence, body and soul, love and lust, candour and falseness, innocence and guilt, pity and cruelty, life and death.

Talking about *Hamlet*

In spite of the length, the frequency of language difficulties, the complexity and diversity of its concerns, the young are not afraid of this play. Students, like all of us, willingly join the stage-people in their constant preoccupation: Where is Hamlet? How is he? What is he about? What is he concealing? What does he mean? Send for him, seek him, find him, sift him. The play is as good as a thesaurus for locutions connoting inquiry.

Talking about *Hamlet* is not a problem. The difficulty is to fit in all that everyone wants to say. One of the consequences of the energetic curiosity the play releases is that discussions frequently break away from the structure intended at the outset. However, since there is always a great deal of doubling back, most of the questions are eventually touched on. Generally, it works best to have a set of aspects in mind, but to let what happens during one discussion determine which aspect is taken up in the next. To make this freedom of movement possible, the discussions do not begin until the students have reread the whole play privately.

"*There needs no ghost . . .*"

The ghost is a natural starting-point. An interesting comment on the great diversity of idea and action in the play is that the events of the first act sometimes appear to have been forgotten by the end of the play-reading. The killing of the King is taken as something that was bound to happen sooner or later, ghost or no ghost, given the intensity of Hamlet's hatred and the King's treachery.

Discussion points: Irruption from another order of existence. The acceptance by the sentries and Horatio. The revelations; the ambiguity of the Queen's guilt; the commandment. The puzzle of the 'cellarage' sequence.

"My father's spirit": Hamlet's moral and intellectual acceptance. "A questionable shape". Doubt then or only later? His reaction to the Ghost in the Closet scene.

"More things in heaven and earth": The two worlds of the Battlement scenes. Double reality throughout the play. The dimension of religion. Divinity and Fate. Hamlet's belief in a higher order.

(The discussion which follows might be concerned with the visible reality invaded by the Ghost.)

"*Denmark's a prison*"

Vividness of the everyday routine at Elsinore. The mixture of public and family affairs in the King's opening speech. (Notice the quantity of terms for family relationships in I.ii.) The mixture throughout the play. (This might include some talk of the impression that *Hamlet* is full of topical references, most of which are now lost.)

The King's Denmark: The King as ruler. The moral code of the court. The King's 'sponges'. Corruption at Elsinore and the effect on the whole state. Disease imagery.

Hamlet's Denmark: Hamlet's criticism of the court. His knowledge of "the distracted multitude". His extreme responsiveness to every sort of experience. How much of the Denmark outside the court is made present through his use of ordinary life as the chief source of imagery.

(This discussion might be followed by examination of the language-scape of the play, or of the shaping of the action, or of the quality of Hamlet's mind.)

"*Words, words, words*"

The flow of talk in that articulate court. Signs of a common training in rhetoric. Any exceptions? The fondness for clever talk. The purposes of language; rhetoric and deception.

"More matter with less art." Is tediousness confined to Polonius? Does the audience find Polonius tedious?

"He that plays the King": The King's language-mask. What happens when he takes it off—if he ever does?

The balance of discourse and rapid cross-talk. Hamlet as the source of variety of language in the play. The different registers he commands according to the immediate demands of the situation.

What will Hamlet say now? as a source of continual surprise throughout. The vigour of his rhetoric; his gift for lively images.

The "To be or not to be" soliloquy as an example of living correspondence between expression and movement of thought.

Hamlet as a hero who is also the Fool(**54**). The amount of fooling in the tragedy. Only the result of the "antic disposition" or a natural part of Hamlet's energy of response?

"To hold the mirror up to Nature"

Amount of theatrical information in the play(**55**). Dramatic effect of the play-within-a-play. Hamlet as actor. Directions to Burbage.

Smoothness and variety of action—from scene to scene, within a scene. (Good for illustrations: II.ii; III.i; III.iv; IV.v.) Naturalness of encounters. The way scenes start.

Effect of Elsinore setting. Significance of placing of the scenes which are set outside the castle.

Hamlet and the action—controller or controlled? The action as following the course of a duel between the King and Hamlet.

Suspense. Test the suggestion that Hamlet never fails to surprise the audience. (To examine a scene chosen at random makes clear the marvellous contextual timing throughout the play.) Is Hamlet himself ever surprised by events?

Hamlet's alert consciousness as compelling the audience to enter what they watch. The soliloquies—inside or outside the action? (The well-known puzzles of what happens in *Hamlet* usually come up without prompting at various points during the discussions or in the *Notes for a new production*.)

"As swift as meditation or the thoughts of love"

The speed of Hamlet's thinking. (Examine some instances such as what is happening in his mind while listening to the Player; to the report of the Ghost's appearance. The leaps of thought in the Prayer scene.)

Contrast with the pace of the shrewd King's thinking.

Acuteness of Hamlet's judgement of men and manners. Give examples. Source and consequences of his errors of judgement.

"Let me not burst in ignorance." Intellectual curiosity. The range of knowledge and interests. The fascination with the mystery of the human condition.

Marks of scholarly training in questions and speculation, even at moments of high emotional tension.

The life of feeling: Strength of Hamlet's emotions. Filial love. Affection for friends. Love for Ophelia. Attitude to sexual love; sources of his revulsion. The passions of the Closet scene. The problem of the Nunnery scene.

Nature of his hatred for the King. Does he show hatred for any other character? Does anyone hate Hamlet?

(The question of the mystery of Hamlet turns up everywhere. The various elements need to be drawn together in the final discussions. Talk about this aspect is least likely to follow an orderly course and never reaches a consensus. At least two periods are necessary.)

"How stand I then?"
Hamlet before the encounter with the Ghost. Nature and depth of his grief. The shock of the Ghost's appearance, revelations, command. Effect on Hamlet's stability. The nature of his madness—real and assumed. Point of restoration.

Significance of indications throughout the play of his past life—childhood, family experience, education, friends, popularity, love. Ophelia's testimony.

"The son of a King": courage, loyalty, conscience, idealism, sense of vocation.

"A mole in nature": pride, cruelty, ruthlessness. Tainted by experience?

"A kind of fighting in my mind": number of fronts he is fighting on—moral, intellectual, spiritual. Pull between the practical demands of the immediate and a larger vision.

"What is a man?": contemplation of life, of death—gift or burden?

"And can say nothing". No one else refers to his delay: why is it so important to him? Admiration for Fortinbras.

"I know my course": moments of decision. How he arrives at a course of action. Out of key with his task or matched to it? "I have cause, and will, and strength, and means." Has he?

Hamlet on himself. Degree of self-knowledge. Admiration for Horatio. The soliloquies—clarification or deepening of the mystery? Does he pluck out the heart of his own mystery?

The end: growth in understanding? Hamlet in the first soliloquy as against Hamlet as he faces the last challenge. Victory or failure?

Versions of Hamlet—from the King, the Queen, Horatio, the audience.

Examining a key scene

In the great plays scenes occur which strike us with special intensity, which so possess imagination that the key to understanding seems within reach. It seems then that we do for a moment know the play not as spectators but as sharers in the action. Such scenes make very clear the power of the dramatic form for putting it all *before* us, literally presenting suffering flesh and blood. The vision of these moments lights up the whole play. Indeed, the whole seems to be contained there. The effect is to quicken our capacity to see not only the immediate event, but also what has happened and what has yet to happen. To explore one such scene is an essential part of the preparation for individual work.

King Lear IV. vii

Discussion might begin with recalling the restlessness of the play, the continuous agitation of action and counter-action. I should pick up the

Fool's "Let go thy hold when a great wheel runs down a hill lest thou break thy neck with following", to introduce the notion of this scene as the still point at the centre of the wheel.

Preparation for the scene in the preceding action: The signs of hope in the first five scenes of Act IV. Gloucester in Edgar's care (sc. i); Albany's recognition and rejection of evil (sc. ii); the vulgarity of Goneril and Regan (scs. ii and v); Cordelia herself (sc. iv). The violent contrasts of sc. vi: the upward movement continued in Gloucester's rescue and the plunge into torment when Lear is at last on the stage again. Can anything redeem this pain?

1–20 Effect on audience of the quiet exchanges between Cordelia and Kent; the phrase "the modest truth"; the question waited for, "How does the King?" and the answer, "Sleeps still". Heightening of suspense in Cordelia's prayer and against that the words "fresh garments" and the surprise of the Doctor's term for Lear—"temperance".

21–44 The gradual movement inwards: cf I. i. Intimate contact between Lear and Cordelia at the centre of each scene. Stage-picture echo of I. i—the entry of the king and the immediate turning of attention towards him. Significant difference: Lear now surrounded only by good (cf "her kind nursery"); the open air setting.

The first gesture—Cordelia's embrace of the sleeping Lear. (This is the first of the three embraces specified in the play. The other two are Lear's embrace of Cordelia in the Captivity scene—"Ha, have I caught thee?"—and his embrace of Cordelia dead.) Cordelia's evocation of the previous action: the depth of the bond between father and child conveyed in her echoing of Lear's own speech. What Cordelia stands for here. Interruption of the flow of rhetoric by Lear's stirring. Move from symbol to daughter—Cordelia at a loss for words, the stiffness of the words she finds.

45–68 The entirely natural slowness with which Lear's blurred mind comes to clarity. Unexpectedness of the first words; shock of "I am bound upon a wheel of fire". Where is Lear now? Do we know what he sees when he uses the words "a soul in bliss", "a spirit"? Can even Cordelia follow him into the depths?

The effort of returning consciousness—the three questions, the testing of his body. cf I. iv 235–237.

The second gesture—Lear's kneeling. Meaning left open: what is Lear kneeling to—"a soul in bliss"? his wronged child? the gods? Why are his next words "Pray, do not mock me"?

Returning sanity: self-identification. "A very foolish fond old man." Compare *who* he is I. iv. Acknowledgement of uncertainty—frequency of word "know" in the scene; the little certainties of judgement—place, garments, immediate past.

68–85 Release of feeling: simple naming—"my child Cordelia"; Cordelia's simple affirmation.

The third gesture—Lear's hand touching Cordelia's face. How does this affect our reaction to his sliding out of reach again? Does he hear Cordelia's "no cause, no cause"? Echo in word "cause"? Irony of his recalling now his other daughters. Audience knowledge thus invoked—connection between Lear's present state and Goneril's and Regan's view of him?

Lear's royalty: how is it present in the scene? Is it part of what Lear recalls? Significance of what parts of the past he recalls?

Lowering of tension: entry of Kent and the Doctor into the dialogue; "the great rage,/You *see*, is kill'd in him."

The unburthening: "Will't please your Highness walk?" Recall the first time we heard Lear's voice—"unburthen'd crawl towards death". Difference of the present unburthening? Recall the earlier struggles for patience. The meaning of patience now? "You must bear with me. Pray you now, forget and forgive: I am old and foolish." What does Lear accept in these words?

86–98 Return of outer world and continuing threat of evil.

Some further questions: The new danger for Lear in what the awakening brings him. The absence in the scene of expression of joy. Cordelia's share in the dialogue; connection with her inability to "heave her heart into her mouth". The ways in which the Fool and his knowledge are present in the scene. How the Awakening scene and the last scene contain one another.

Macbeth III. ii

When the scene opens, we already know how achieved ambition tastes to Macbeth; we know nothing of Lady Macbeth's state. Discussion might begin with recalling the way her role has been handled up to now; her sudden appearance in I. v; the strength of her constant partnership of Macbeth in planning and execution of the murder; the slightness of her presence since then.

The two characters

The effect of evil within each. Common despair and ambition for death. Lady Macbeth's emptiness of purpose; Macbeth's distorted purpose. Her attempt to deaden consciousness; "thoughts that should have died". Connection with her behaviour in the Murder scene and her eventual madness. His full consciousness of the inescapable "torture of the mind". Macbeth's language as showing him poised between sanity and madness. The course each is now set on.

The light the placing of the scene throws on the degree of Lady Macbeth's responsibility in the choice of evil: the categorical exclusion from the "deed of dreadful note" against how the stage-picture recalls the weight of her share in the initial choice. Significance of Macbeth's now using the serpent image first heard from her, and the associated "O full of scorpions is my mind, dear wife". Later echoes—"There the grown serpent lies" and "cleanse the stuff'd bosom of that perilous stuff . . .". What other image does Macbeth now take over from Lady Macbeth? The relationship between them. Failure of contact now and elsewhere. What binds them now?

Appearance and reality
The scene as sustained irony exploring the assertion, "what's done is done". The current of appearance/reality allusions, of images of distortion. The apparent intimacy and real separation of the two characters. The epitaph on Duncan recalling the earlier, "Had I but died an hour before this chance . . .". How, in both instances, is what is said both true and false at once?

Dialogue as appearance
How often is Macbeth aware of a hearer? Actual and virtual soliloquy up to this moment. Significance of the fact that the last of the actual soliloquies occurs in the preceding scene. Connection between the distortion of the conventions of dramatic speech and the effect of evil.

Echo
The scene as a paradigm of the shaping device of the play—exploitation of echo. Density of the major images and iterations here—murdered sleep, broken world, disguise, black agents, nature, death, poison, fear, the serpent, the bell, the blood, the dark, the king among his subjects. The scene as the gathering point of the echoes. Implications of this, given the stage-picture, for the source of evil in the play.

Action
Absence of significant event in the scene. Connection between this and the two planes of action in the play, inner and outer. Connection between non-action and the state of damnation. Where in the play is Macbeth *seen* performing an act?

Why this scene at all? Only for the sake of the poetry? What would be lost in cutting it? Set the Macbeth of this scene against the Macbeth of "She should have died hereafter . . .".

Pattern and meaning

Grappling with the meanings of certain plays prescribed at senior level depends on recognition of their emblematic pattern. *King Lear*, *The Tempest*, *The Winter's Tale* are examples. Reading these plays with a new audience makes one sharply aware of how distorting an influence the 19th-century novel has on what is expected from Shakespeare. What is actually happening in the play may be lost sight of because it does not match a preconception of what should happen in a story. To counter this unprofitable way of response, it is the idea of the play that needs to be restored. Shakespeare was a dramatist exploring the possibilities of the stage spectacle, not of the novel. 'Most *difficulties*—of structure, of plot credibility, of tangled speech, or anything else—are immediately resolved by the simple expedient of mentally putting the plays upon the stage' **(56)**. Emblem is a vital element in these plays: it is through watching emblem in action that significance is recognized.

King Lear

In *King Lear*, much depends on how the opening scene is handled during the play-reading stage. The producer aims at making visible the strong ritualistic mode of the scene: the ceremonial entry of the King and the formal arrangement of the "great image of authority" between the opposed figures of truth and falsehood; the love-test, the banishment of the youngest daughter and the loyal servant. It is worth pausing at the end of the scene to make sure that the unambiguous presentation of characters other than Lear has not been missed. Shakespeare spells out very clearly the goodness of Cordelia and Kent and the evil of Goneril and Regan. After the first scene, I should take the play at full speed, and let the powerful activity of theme and emblem work on imagination. 'Significance holds plot and character in an iron grasp'**(57)**. If entry to the play is appropriate, the way is open to consciousness of 'a vision to which the action itself is but a foreground'**(17)**.

With no other tragedy is it so vital for the classroom to remain a rehearsal room during the discussion periods. It is through looking at what the stage is showing, through realizing that speech and action constantly urge us to seeing beyond them, that the disturbing terrors fall into place. Just what aspect of the play to discuss first is a matter of personal choice. One might choose to begin with themes: with responsibility for choice, a man's power to release by a moment's rashness evil forces; or with the bond of love; or with the oppositions between truth and falsehood, selflessness and selfishness, loyalty and treachery, reason and madness, and so on. My own preference is to start with the doubleness of everything: the shadow plot which holds the audience relentlessly within the play; the investing of characters with double roles—King and Madman, Fool and Sage, Beggar and Champion, and so on; incident which is actual and emblematic at once—Storm, Journey, Trial, Recognition, Captivity.

It is through Lear himself that the doubleness is most profoundly realized, and all discussions lead to Lear as the centre of both the actuality of the foreground and the 'extra-theatrical truth'. What one would want students to see is that he is at all points both a man with a unique personal history and everyman with a common history. Sympathy with Lear is sympathy with the particularity of human suffering, human folly, human need, human bewilderment. Pity is roused by the sight of "the thing itself". So it is the individualization which is first explored—the quick explosions, extravagant gestures, demands for attention, astonishing candour in sanity as well as in madness, and most of all, the gift for speech from the heart at moments of highest feeling. Lear gains as much wisdom as a man can gain, without losing a jot of his individuality. His last act insists on this truth of the play: "I killed the slave that was a-hanging thee." And it is Lear, the only highly individualized character, who constantly urges on us the significance of his role. He questions the "cause in nature", pierces disguises, challenges elements and gods, preaches sermons, enters hell, takes on himself "the mystery of things". His simplest utterances open a shaft to the depths of experience.

The Tempest and *The Winter's Tale*

In the last plays, Shakespeare exploits theatrical artifice to a much greater extent than elsewhere in the canon. This feature makes seeing before reading the ideal way of meeting *The Tempest* and *The Winter's Tale*. This ideal is rarely attainable, which makes it specially important that the play-reading be dramatically visible. I should introduce these plays as a fresh experiment—the great playwright at the end of his career still testing the reach of his craft. The new theatre at Blackfriars probably had something to do with the new artifice. Here was a different kind of theatre from the Globe: an indoor theatre with a smaller stage and auditorium, sophisticated lighting, more elaborate machinery **(50)**.

The play-reading would be a discovery of Shakespeare's discovery of yet another way of tilting the mirror. During the reading there would be comment from producer and students on the emerging patterns.

In *The Tempest*: the meticulous structure; patterns of action and character moving to completeness within a precisely measured frame; the narrow time-scale so unlike that of any other play and yet accommodating the time of generations; the artificiality of the island within which "all of us [find] ourselves".

In *The Winter's Tale*: the expansive three-part structure; the unexpected linking and overlapping of tragedy and romance; the realisms, both comic and tragic, and the pastoral grace; the theatricality of the pursuing bear and the living statue**(58)**. With *The Winter's Tale* it is worth making sure that the ending is the surprise it is in the theatre for a spectator who does not know the play. I should time the reading so that the last two scenes are read in the same period. Production of the Recognition scene would stress the rapid naturalness of it, the sense of happy public excitement and satisfaction. This prepares for the different rhythms of the Statue scene, the dignified withdrawal which culminates in the solemn wonder.

Discussion of these plays might begin with recapitulation of the elements of the surface pattern and then move into the pattern of ideas which sustains the surface. For instance, the love-stories in the first two parts of *The Winter's Tale* present two contrasting surface patterns: the court tale of harmony disintegrating from within and the tragic conclusion; the country tale of harmony resisting the threat from without and the promise of fulfilment. Links between the surfaces are identified; Leontes's causeless jealousy, Polixenes's inconsistent rejection of the grafting of Florizel and Perdita; the diseased excitement of Leontes's description of what Hermione does ("Is whispering nothing ..."), the healthy excitement of Florizel's description of what Perdita does ("What you do/ Still betters what is done ..."); Mamilius's death, Perdita's rescue; Hermione's mature superiority, Perdita's youthful superiority; the happy frankness of both Hermione and Perdita. It will be noticed that this set of links is itself linked by the fact of change. The first link contains the change of Polixenes from suffering tyranny to inflicting it; the second contains the change from death to life. (Hermione is 'dead' at this stage.) Thus, identifying the surface patterns would lead to discussion of the interplay of ideas of transformation and renewal.

In *The Tempest*, the element of suspended action in the surface pattern might be a starting-point for discussion of emblematic significance in the play. This thread of "rough magic" runs from I. ii to V. i: Miranda's sleep, the sleep of the ship's company, the binding of Ferdinand, the sleep of Alonzo and company in the Banquet magic, the charming of Alonzo and company in the circle. The device is effective theatre, which charms audience as well as characters. Reflection on the different instances leads to appreciation of the device as emblem. Miranda's sleep was no doubt prompted by the need to get her out of the way for the dialogue with Ariel, but Shakespeare makes it serve other purposes too. Prospero's magic here is unambiguously beneficent: the sleep is "a good dullness". There is humour in it, considering the length and difficulty of her father's discourse. The sleep of the ship's company may be seen as simply convenient for the plot, but the sleep of Alonzo and Gonzalo again serves a deeper purpose, more complex than in Miranda's case. Gonzalo's goodness and Alonzo's potential redemption are implied by the fact that they can sleep, Antonio's and Sebastian's evil is implied by the fact that they can't. Inaction is thus set against "open-eyed conspiracy". There is another twist: Gonzalo's waking leads to a *natural* case of suspended action in Antonio and Sebastian. Natural goodness, if it is vigilant, can overcome the threat of evil. Gonzalo's waking is thus linked with Prospero's unceasing vigilance and with the eventual abjuration of "rough magic". The cases of sword-binding again prompt reflection on inaction and action. Ferdinand's inaction frees him to accept the action of service, and is rewarded by fulfilment of desire. Alonzo's inaction enables him to hear the rebuke of his conscience. Inaction bears no fruit in Antonio and Sebastian. There is unregenerate evil, which can be controlled but not transformed by the effects of goodness; what follows the last charm makes this clear.

How far one can go in discussion of significance in these plays depends on the sophistication of the class. Naturally, only a fraction of the complex design can be dealt with. The aim of discussion is certainly not to develop a theory of the play's meaning, but to awaken responsiveness to the idea-activity "beating in [the] mind".

Notes for a new production

To grapple independently with the meanings of the play is the challenge set by *Notes for a new production.* Each student reads the play as if he has been given the chance to produce it and keeps a systematic record of his thinking. Envisaging a production means that imaginative response keeps pace with intellectual inquiry. The challenge allows students of different ability to reach their own level of understanding: there is firm working-ground for all students and plenty of scope for the exceptional ones. The work fully meets exam requirements: material for answering questions is assembled in an organized manner; memory is sharpened by the personal responsibility involved; secondary reading, if it is being done, has a definable purpose.

When and where the work is done depends on school organization. Generally, students choose their own time; but there should, I think, be some class-periods given to the project, during which students may work privately or talk about their problems to one another or to the teacher. A great advantage of these periods is that they allow for that invaluable contact between teacher and individual student for which it is so often difficult to find room.

It is *notes*, not a full-scale plan of production, which is in question. The 'producers' are not being asked to find solutions for technical problems of staging—the shipwreck in *The Tempest*, the bear in *The Winter's Tale*, Gloucester's attempted suicide. The emphasis is on meaning. For instance, whether Banquo's ghost enters or not is a legitimate problem; how he enters (if he does), or what to use for his "gory locks" is not. Again, where a scene takes place may be important, but this does not demand a description of the set. The question of a set for the whole production is left to the end. An interesting exercise is then to write a note for the stage designer, indicating the kind of set which would best serve the producer's interpretation.

To help students read closely, it is worth providing them with a set of points to keep in mind such as the following:

Watch for Shakespeare's own directions *within* as well as beside the text. Keep your imagination open for what the words are making visible on the bare boards—evocation of atmosphere, of place, indication of gesture, of a character's way of moving and speaking. (For example, the blind Gloucester identifies Lear by "that trick of the voice". What is that trick? Listen for it throughout.)

Try to discover the logic of scene-sequence. Pay special attention to the way the big scenes are mounted.

Watch how characters come into the light, how main characters establish their identity, how knowledge deepens on each appearance.

Watch the timing of revelation. (For example, Iago's enjoyment of his evil designs is implicit from the beginning; it is not explicit till the end of II. iv.)

Remember that characters are always in action and interaction. When a group is on the stage, visualize their awareness of one another. Do all the characters attend to and hear everything that is said? When a character makes an entrance in the middle of a scene, try to pick up his reading of the situation he finds. (For example, what does Macbeth see when he enters in I. v?) When a character is alone, remember that the whole play is around him.

Language is a vital part of character in action. Watch in particular the language the hero uses; plainness and richness, eloquence and inarticulateness, obscurity and directness. When a character surprises you, think whether the surprise is out of character or a new revelation. (For example, Desdemona's dialogue with Iago II. i. Hamlet springs several surprises.)

Watch for connections through which themes come constantly to life—images, echoes, parallels, ironies.

Try charting the emotional pattern in big scenes. Try pacing some of the big speeches—pitch, stressing, pause. (For example, how would your Hamlet deliver the "Angels and ministers of grace defend us" speech? Reverently? excitedly? rapidly? slowly? incredulously? fearfully? a mixture of the lot?)

Sometimes, when you have read a scene, isolate a line at random and decide how you would want your actor to speak it. (For example, what significance would you want Othello's "That's a fault" to convey? When Lear says, "I can be patient; I can stay with Regan ...", would each 'can' have the same weight?)

At moments of high drama, where are a character's eyes? (For example, where does Othello look during the "magic in the web" sequence?)

Listen to the poetry. When would you warn your actors not to get in Shakespeare's way?

The suggestions above would need modification for *The Winter's Tale* and *The Tempest*. There would be less emphasis on exploration of character and more on what a character stands for, less on individuality and more on archetypal qualities.

Sample extract from notes on *Hamlet* II. ii—Players' entry to end

Stage-picture: Arrival of Players gives Hamlet a chance to escape from the court people. He goes into the middle of the new arrivals, separating himself from Polonius, Rosencrantz and Guildenstern. His answers to Polonius's interruptions are shouted across the stage. Rosencrantz and Guildenstern watch Hamlet all the time. Bring this out by putting them at two different places on the stage to watch him.

Hamlet with the Players: Relaxed, not on his guard. Impression of his old life, especially with the First Player, his "old friend". "If it live in your memory . . ."—reminder of what lives in Hamlet's memory. cf I. v "while memory holds a seat . . ."

The Pyrrhus speech: Hamlet speaks for the Players, not for the courtiers. He becomes a player himself. From "the blood of fathers" on, he is caught up in his own acting, he keeps looking at the First Player. He doesn't hear Polonius's applause. The First Player takes over without a break. Hamlet stands still until Polonius's "This is too long". That breaks the spell. Hamlet moves so that his face is turned away from the audience during the Hecuba speech. Player has "tears in his eyes . . . a broken voice".

Clearing of stage: Hamlet keeps his distance, calls out instructions—"Do you hear?"—to Polonius. Talk with First Player about *The Murder of Gonzago*. Makes audience curious with talk of writing a speech. When the Player has left, Hamlet starts towards the audience, stops when he sees Rosencrantz and Guildenstern. "My good friends", etc. barely conceals that he wants to get rid of them. "Good my lord"—they move towards him, but he points after Polonius and the Players and waits for them to go. Then he comes straight at the audience. "Now I am *alone*"—for the first time in Act II.

Third soliloquy: "O what a rogue and peasant slave am I". First chance since the Ghost scene to find out what is really going on inside Hamlet. Everyone in the court thinks he is mad. Is he? What about the "antic disposition"? What was he thinking during the Hecuba speech? What has happened to the revenge he was going to "*sweep* to"? I. iv.

First his speech is rapid and confused. He 'unpacks' his heart with *words*, but how much does he reveal in the rush of questions? cf "wild and whirling words" I. v. Excited by the Player's *words*. Note "and can *say* nothing". He seems to see language as action, to think using "horrid speech" his duty.

He thinks of his father "upon whose property, and most dear life,/A damn'd attack was made", but changes to an attack on his own cowardice. Acting a new part that no one believes in.

His attack on the King is vicious, blazing hatred, stronger than earlier attacks in the Ghost scene. As in the first soliloquy, there is sexual disgust—"bawdy", "lecherous". He sees the King in his 'mind's eye', and this brings him to a halt. He sees himself and his acting and invites the audience to despise it too. He is no better than a "whore", a "scullion".

"About my brain": suspense. What will he do now? After that pause his speech is cold and clear.

Plan for play a surprise after the cry "O vengeance". Sees the play already in the 'mind's eye'. What is he about? Surely he does "know his course". What does he doubt, himself or the justice of the Ghost's command?

Now he pulls back from the audience. Last lines are real thinking aloud, let us in on his thoughts rather than just his feelings. His mind jumps to the idea that "the spirit may be the devil", and on to the idea that it may be tempting him to ruin. Or has he been thinking this all the time? "The play's the thing": Is this an effort to persuade himself that he needs proof or a real belief that he hasn't enough evidence, or a desire "to catch the *conscience* of the King"?

"My weakness and my melancholy": Himself unsure of his sanity.

What do we learn? At ease with the Players and they with him. Excited by the Player's speech, horrified by his own inaction, unsure of his courage, maddened by hatred. He thinks up a cunning plot, fears for the state of his soul, is troubled by doubts.

Shakespeare in the classroom begins with the teacher as producer; it ends with the students trying the role themselves. *Notes for a new production* is not an attempt to train literary critics, but a way of developing the skill to be an active audience. It is an invitation to give close attention to something already enjoyed. "Approach to the meaning restores the experience in another dimension"**(59)**. The hope is that students will find the exercise as exciting as the original experience of the play is entertaining.

References

Chapter One

1 Granville-Barker, H. Letter to John Gielgud. Quoted by Trewin in *Shakespeare on the English Stage*(12).
2 Brown, John Russell. *Shakespeare's Plays in Performance*, Arnold, 1966.
3 Brown, John Russell. *Discovering Shakespeare*, Macmillan, 1981.
4 Coghill, Neville. *Shakespeare's Professional Skills*, Cambridge U.P., 1964.
5 David, Richard. *Shakespeare in the Theatre*, Cambridge U.P., 1978.
6 Muir, Kenneth. *Shakespeare the Professional*, Heinemann, 1973.
7 Ripley, John. '*Julius Caesar*' *on Stage in England and America*, Cambridge U.P., 1980.
8 Rosenberg, Marvin. *The Masks of Othello*, 1961; *The Masks of King Lear*, 1972; *The Masks of Macbeth*, 1978, University of California Press.
9 Speaight, Robert. *Shakespeare on the Stage*, Collins, 1973.
10 Sprague, A. C. *Shakespeare and the Actors 1660–1905*, Harvard U.P., 1944.
11 Styan, J. L. *Shakespeare's Stagecraft*, Cambridge U.P., 1967.
12 Trewin, J. *Shakespeare on the English Stage 1900–1964*, Barrie and Rockliff, 1964.
13 Wells, Stanley. *Royal Shakespeare*, Manchester U.P., 1977.
14 For information about services offered by the RSC, write to *RSC Development Administrator*, *Royal Shakespeare Theatre*, *Stratford-upon-Avon CV37 6BB*.
15 Eliot, T. S. 'Dante', *Selected Essays*, Faber, 1951.
16 Darlington, W. A. *The Daily Telegraph*, quoted by Trewin in *Shakespeare on the English Stage* (12).

Chapter Two

17 Granville-Barker, H. *Prefaces to Shakespeare*, 2 vols. Batsford, 1958: always stimulating for the teacher/producer.

Chapter Three

18 Ellis-Fermor, Una. *Shakespeare the Dramatist*, Methuen, 1962.
19 Welsford, Enid. *The Fool*, Faber, 1935.
20 Jenkins, Harold. 'As You Like It', *Shakespeare Survey 8*, Cambridge U.P., 1955; excellent essay on the way the play is made.
21 Hollander, John. 'The Role of Music in *Twelfth Night*', *Twelfth Night: a Casebook*, Macmillan, 1972.
22 Evans, Bertrand. 'The Fruits of the Sport', *ibid.*: a lively account of how Shakespeare handles the "bundles of awarenesses" in *Twelfth Night*.
23 See Bradbrook, M. C. 'The Sources of *Macbeth*', *Shakespeare Survey 4*.
24 Clemen, W. H. *The Development of Shakespeare's Imagery*, Methuen, 1951.

Chapter Four

25 Wilson, F. P. *Shakespearian and Other Studies*, Oxford, Clarendon Press, 1969.
26 Brown, Arthur. 'Shakespeare's Treatment of Comedy', *Shakespeare's World*, ed. Sutherland, J. and Hurstfield, J., Arnold, 1964.
27 There is a good section on the possible interpretations in *Shakespeare's Plays in Performance* (2).
28 See Bradbrook, M. C. 'The New Clown: *Twelfth Night*', *Shakespeare the Craftsman*, Chatto and Windus, 1969.
29 *Shakespearean Songs and Lute Solos*, The Deller Consort, Oryx 1526.
30 Reese, M. M. *The Cease of Majesty*, Arnold, 1961.
31 M. C. Bradbrook has a helpful essay on this subject in *Manner and Meaning in Shakespeare*, ed. Jackson, B. A. W., McMaster U.P. and Irish U.P., 1969.
32 Wilson, J. Dover. 'The Elizabethan Shakespeare', *Romeo and Juliet, Twentieth Century Interpretations*, Prentice-Hall, 1970.
33 Gibbons, Brian. Introduction, *Romeo and Juliet*, Arden edition 1980.
34 Recordings of *Romeo and Juliet*: Marlowe Dramatic Society, Argo ZPR 208/211. Caedmon SRS 228 has Edith Evans playing the Nurse.
35 Muir, Kenneth. *Shakespeare's Comic Sequence*, Liverpool U.P., 1979.
36 Gardner, Helen. 'As You Like It', *More Talking of Shakespeare*, ed. Garrett, John, Longman, 1959.

Chapter Five

37 Leech, Clifford. *'Twelfth Night' and Shakespearian Comedy*, University of Toronto Press, 1965.
38 Lawlor, John. *The Tragic Sense in Shakespeare*, Chatto and Windus, 1960.
39 Knights, L. C. *Some Shakespearean Themes*, Chatto and Windus 1959.
40 Bacon, Francis. See Sylvester, David. *Interviews with Francis Bacon*, Thames and Hudson, 1980.
41 Heilman, R. B. *This Great Stage*, University of Washington Press, 1947.
42 Knights, L. C. 'The Question of Character in Shakespeare', *More Talking of Shakespeare* (36).
43 Storey, Graham. 'The Success of *Much Ado about Nothing*', *ibid.*
44 Knights, L. C. 'The Teaching of Shakespeare', *Manner and Meaning in Shakespeare* (31).
45 Nowottny, Winifred. 'Shakespeare's Tragedies', *Shakespeare's World* (26).
46 For a study of the relationship between imagery and meaning, see Clemen (24). Particularly good on Hamlet's language.
47 Lascelles, Mary. 'Shakespeare's Pastoral Comedy', *More Talking of Shakespeare* (36).
48 Some sources of information: Reese, M. M. *Shakespeare, His World and His Work*, Arnold, 1953; Muir, Kenneth and Schoenbaum, S. ed. *A New Companion to Shakespeare Studies*, Cambridge U.P., 1971; Nicoll, Allardyce. *Shakespeare in His Own Age, Shakespeare Survey 17*, 1964.
49 Whitehead, A. N. *The Aims of Education*, Benn, 1962.
50 Nagler, A. M. *Shakespeare's Stage*, Yale U.P., 1958: a good short account of the subject. See also (48).
51 Studies of individual plays are found in: *Studies in English Literature*, Arnold; *Notes on English Literature*, Blackwell; *Critical Commentaries*, Macmillan.
52 Collections of extracts useful for introducing students to leading critics: *The*

Casebook Series, Macmillan; *Twentieth Century Interpretations*, Prentice-Hall; *Shakespeare's Tragedies* and *Shakespeare's Comedies*, ed. Lerner, L., Penguin.
53 Muir, Kenneth. *Shakespeare's Tragic Sequence*, Liverpool U.P., 1979.
54 See Levin, Harry. 'The Antic Disposition', *Hamlet, A Casebook*, Macmillan, 1968.
55 See Bradbrook, M. C. 'Old things made new: *Hamlet, Prince of Denmark*' (28).
56 Pafford, J. H. P. Introduction to *The Winter's Tale*, Arden edition, 1963.
57 Mack, Maynard. *King Lear in Our Time*, Methuen, 1966.
58 Two excellent essays on the stagecraft of *The Winter's Tale*: 'Six Points of Stagecraft in *The Winter's Tale*', by Nevill Coghill, *Shakespeare Survey 11*; 'Some Dramatic Techniques in *The Winter's Tale*' by William H. Matchett, *Shakespeare Survey 22*.
59 Eliot, T. S. *Four Quartets*.

Index